Math in Focus®
Singapore Math®
by Marshall Cavendish®

GRADE 3A

Workbook

Consultant and Author
Dr. Fong Ho Kheong

Authors
Chelvi Ramakrishnan and Michelle Choo

U.S. Consultants
Dr. Richard Bisk
Andy Clark
Patsy F. Kanter

 **Marshall Cavendish**
Education

U.S. Distributor

**Houghton
Mifflin
Harcourt**

© 2018 Marshall Cavendish Education Pte Ltd

Published by Marshall Cavendish Education
Times Centre, 1 New Industrial Road, Singapore 536196
Customer Service Hotline: (65) 6213 9688
US Office Tel: (1-914) 332 8888 | Fax: (1-914) 332 8882
E-mail: cs@mceducation.com
Website: www.mceducation.com

Distributed by
Houghton Mifflin Harcourt
222 Berkeley Street
Boston, MA 02116
Tel: 617-351-5000
Website: www.hmheducation.com/mathinfocus

Cover: © Don Hammond/Design Pics/Corbis,
        © Dave Thompson/Life File/Photodisc/Getty Images.
        Images provided by Houghton Mifflin Harcourt.

First published 2018

ISBN 978-1-328-88109-0

Printed in Singapore

6 7 8   1401   23 22 21 20
4500792501   A B C D E

Contents

1 Numbers to 10,000

2 Mental Math and Estimation

Addition up to 10,000

Subtraction up to 10,000

5 Using Bar Models: Addition and Subtraction

6 Multiplication Tables of 6, 7, 8, and 9

7 Multiplication

8 Division

Using Bar Models: Multiplication and Division

Numbers to 10,000

Practice 1 Counting

Write each number shown.

Example

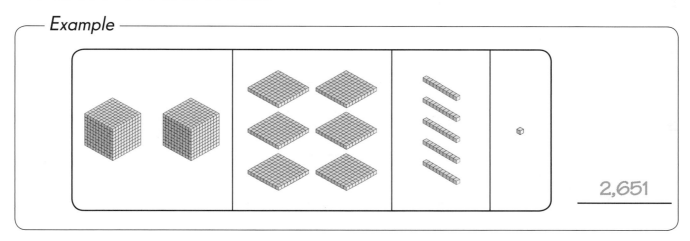

2,651

1.

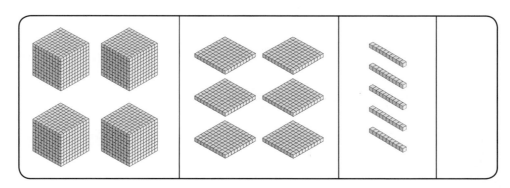

_____

2.

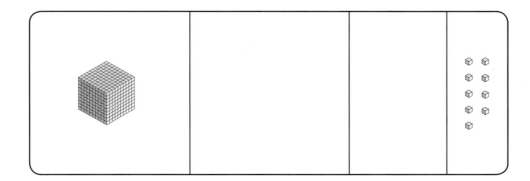

_____

Write each number in word form.

3.  _____

_____

4. _____

_____

5.  _____

_____

6. _____

_____

7.  _____

_____

8. _____

_____

Name: _____   **Date:** _____

Write each number in the box.

9.   nine thousand  **a**

10.   one thousand, four hundred  **o**

11.   six thousand, eight hundred thirty-five  **n**

12.   three thousand, two hundred sixty  **y**

13.   three thousand, two hundred six  **d**

14.   five thousand, sixty-eight  **e**

15.   two thousand, seventy  **k**

16.   five thousand, nine **m**

Match the numbers to the letters.

17.   Who ate the banana?

The _____ _____ _____ _____ _____ _____ ate the banana.
    5,009 1,400 6,835 2,070 5,068 3,260

Count on by ones, tens, hundreds, or thousands.
Fill in the missing numbers.

18. 2,065   2,066   _____   2,068   _____   2,070

19. _____   _____   7,543   7,553   7,563   _____

20. 3,307   3,407   3,507   _____   _____   _____

21. 3,654   4,654   _____   _____   7,654   8,654

Count by tens. Color the rocks the frog jumps on.

22.

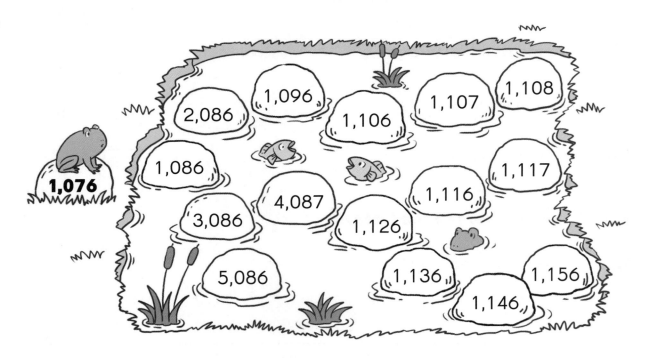

Practice 2 Place Value

Read the numbers on each train. Fill in each blank.

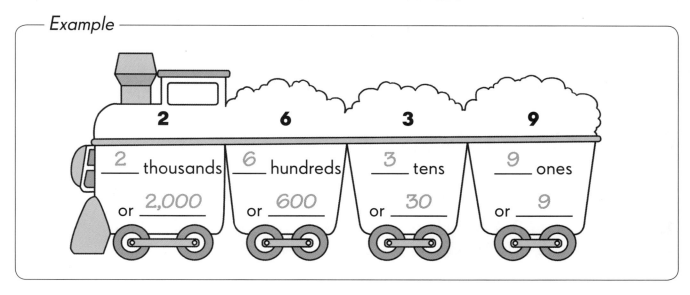

Example

2 6 3 9

_2_ thousands   _6_ hundreds   _3_ tens   _9_ ones

or _2,000_   or _600_   or _30_   or _9_

1.

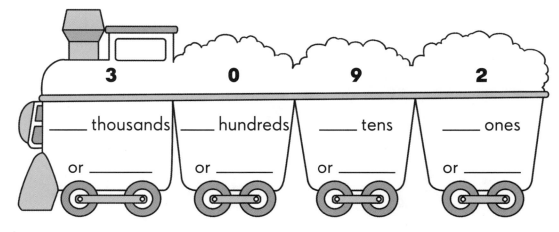

3 0 9 2

___ thousands   ___ hundreds   ___ tens   ___ ones

or ___   or ___   or ___   or ___

2.

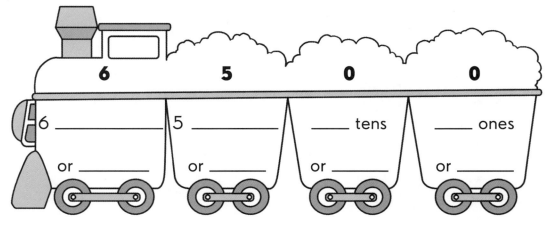

6 5 0 0

6 ___   5 ___   ___ tens   ___ ones

or ___   or ___   or ___   or ___

Write the value of each digit in the box.

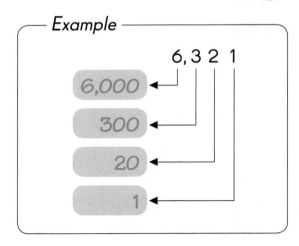

6, 3 2 1

6,000 ←
300 ←
20 ←
1 ←

3.

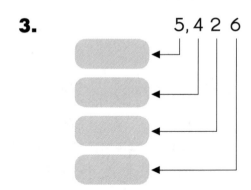

5, 4 2 6

4.

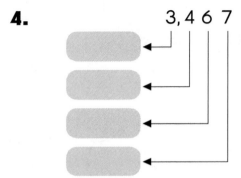

3, 4 6 7

5.

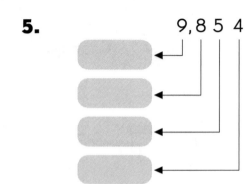

9, 8 5 4

6.

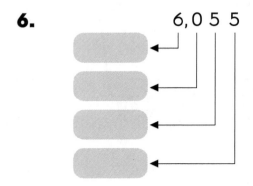

6, 0 5 5

7.

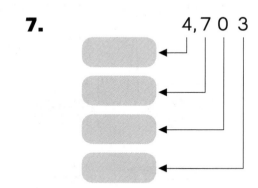

4, 7 0 3

8.

1, 4 2 0

9.

7, 2 9 8

Fill in each blank. Use the place-value chart to help you.

Thousands	Hundreds	Tens	Ones
2	5	4	8

10. In 2,548 the digit 4 is in the _____ place.

The value of the digit is _____.

11. In 2,548 the digit _____ is in the ones place.

The value of the digit is _____.

12. In 2,548 the value of the digit 2 is _____.

It is in the _____ place.

13. In 2,548 the value of the digit _____ is 500.

It is in the _____ place.

Write each number in expanded form, standard form, and word form.

> **Example**
>
> | 7,000 |
> | 200 |
> | 10 |
> | 5 |
>
> $7,215 = 7,000 + 200 + 10 + 5$
>
> 7,215 is the standard form.
>
> Seven thousand, two hundred fifteen is the word form of 7,215.

14.

| 1,000 |
| 600 |
| 40 |
| 3 |

_____ = _____ + _____ + _____ + _____

_____ is the standard form.

_____

is the word form of _____.

Write each number in expanded form, standard form, and word form.

15.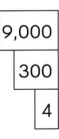

    9,000

      300

        4

_____ = _____ + _____ + _____

_____ is the standard form.

_____

is the word form of _____.

16.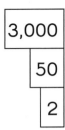

    3,000

      50

       2

_____ = _____ + _____ + _____

_____ is the standard form.

_____

is the word form of _____.

17.

    6,000

      8

_____ = _____ + _____

_____ is the standard form.

_____

is the word form of _____.

18.

    5,000

      800

_____ = _____ + _____

_____ is the standard form.

_____

is the word form of _____.

Write each number shown.

Example

Thousands	Hundreds	Tens	Ones

$6{,}000 + 600 + 40 + 1 =$ ___*6,641*___

6,000, 600, 40, and 1 make ___*6,641*___.

19.

Thousands	Hundreds	Tens	Ones

$2{,}000 + 30 + 4 =$ _____

2,000, 30, and 4 make _____.

20.

Thousands	Hundreds	Tens	Ones

$3{,}000 + 20 =$ _____

3,000 and 20 make _____.

Complete.

21. $7,456 = 7,000 + \underline{\hspace{2cm}} + 50 + 6$

22. $6,391 = 6,000 + 300 + 90 + \underline{\hspace{2cm}}$

23. $6,193 = 6,000 + 100 + \underline{\hspace{2cm}} + 3$

24. $6,107 = 6,000 + 100 + \underline{\hspace{2cm}}$

25. $8,904 = \underline{\hspace{2cm}} + 900 + 4$

26. $5,068 = \underline{\hspace{2cm}} + 60 + 8$

27. $9,074 = 9,000 + \underline{\hspace{2cm}} + 4$

28. $7,005 = 7,000 + \underline{\hspace{2cm}}$

Practice 3 Comparing and Ordering Numbers

Compare. Fill in each blank.

1.   Which number is greater?

Thousands	Hundreds	Tens	Ones
7	5	3	2

Thousands	Hundreds	Tens	Ones
7	3	9	2

_____ is greater than _____.

2.   Which number is less?

Thousands	Hundreds	Tens	Ones
4	5	6	1

Thousands	Hundreds	Tens	Ones
4	5	2	3

_____ is less than _____.

Compare. Write > or < .

3.

4.

5.

6.

Circle the greater number.

7.   8,687   8,987   **8.**   1,251   1,231

Circle the number that is less.

9.   2,012   200   **10.**   7,400   7,402

Circle the greatest number and underline the least number.

11.   6,963   6,639   6,696   6,993

Name: _____   **Date:** _____

Order each set of numbers from least to greatest.

12.   2,340   989   4,001

_____

13.   2,456   1,456   6,456

_____

14.   6,359   6,059   6,759

_____

15.   3,052   3,057   3,050

_____

Order each set of numbers from greatest to least.

16.

 5,317    5,137    5,731   5,713

_____

17.

 3,761    3,671    3,617    3,716

_____

Fill in each blank. Use base-ten blocks to help you.

18.   1 more than 6,348 is _____.

19.   1,000 more than 3,217 is _____.

20.   100 less than 5,608 is _____.

21.   10 less than 2,000 is _____.

Look for a pattern. Fill in the missing numbers.

22.

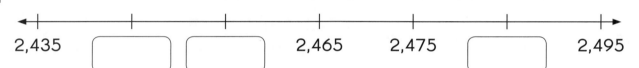

23.

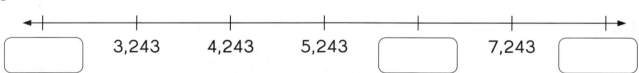

24.

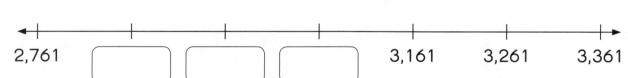

Name: _____   **Date:** _____

Look for a pattern. Fill in the missing numbers.

25.

3,515   4,515   [ ]   [ ]   7,515   [ ]   9,515

26.

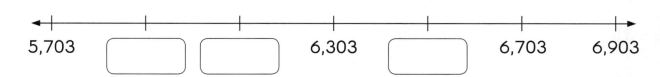

5,703   [ ]   [ ]   6,303   [ ]   6,703   6,903

27.

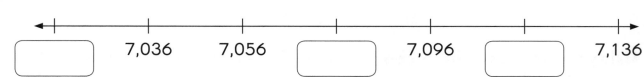

[ ]   7,036   7,056   [ ]   7,096   [ ]   7,136

Complete each number pattern.

28. _____ _____ _____ 5,755   5,765   5,775

29. 8,625   8,725 _____ _____ 9,025   9,125

30. 862   962 _____ 1,162   1,262 _____

31. 6,315   6,215   6,115 _____ _____ _____

Help Sam follow the correct numbers on the map to get to his mother's office. Write your answers in the boxes.

32. Which is the least: 3,456   8,265   or   4,456?

33. Which is the greatest: 1,978   1,987   or   1,889?

34. Complete the number pattern.

1,980   1,990 _____ 2,010

35. Which is less: 8,219 or 8,291?

36. 100 more than 1,912 is _____ .

37. What number is missing?

1,901   1,900   _____   1,898

Using the numbers in the boxes, color the route that Sam takes to his mother's office.

38. Which office building does he go to?   Office Building [   ]

Name: _____ Date: _____

Put On Your Thinking Cap!

Challenging Practice

Write the missing number in the pattern.

1.

Thousands	Hundreds	Tens	Ones
5	6	2	3
6	6	2	2
7	6	2	1
8			

Complete each number pattern.

2. 5,621   5,741   5,861   5,8̶0̶7̶   5,981

3. 6,871   5,861   4,_____   3,841

4. 2,828   2,818   2,808   _____

Fill in the mystery numbers.

5. I am a 3-digit number. The digit in my tens and ones places is the same. The digit in my hundreds place is 4 more than the digit in my tens and ones places.

I am _____.

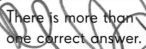

There is more than one correct answer.

6
5

7
6
1

Put On Your Thinking Cap!

Problem Solving

I am a 4-digit number.

The digit 8 is in the hundreds place.

The digit in the thousands place is greater than the digit in the hundreds place.

The digit in the ones place is the smallest possible digit.

The digit in the tens place is 3 less than 6.

What number am I?

_4_

Chapter 2 Mental Math and Estimation

Practice 1   Mental Addition

Add mentally. First, add the tens. Then, add the ones.

> *Example*
>
> 37 + 52 = ?
>
> 37 + 50 = ___*87*___
>
> ___*87*___ + ___*2*___ = ___*89*___
>
> So, 37 + 52 = ___*89*___.
>
>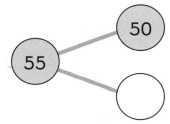
>
> First, add 50. Then, add 2.

1.   24 + 55 = ?

24 + 50 = _____

_____ + _____ = _____

So, 24 + 55 = _____.

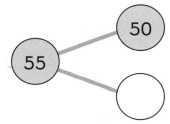

2.   22 + 64 = ?

20 + 64 = _____

_____ + _____ = _____

So, 22 + 64 = _____.

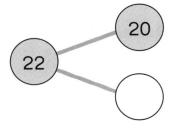

Add mentally. First, add the tens. Then, subtract the extra ones.

Example

19 + 58 = ?

19 + 60 = _____79_____

_____79_____ − _____2_____ = _____77_____

So, 19 + 58 = _____77_____.

First, add 60.
Then, subtract 2.

60 — 58
   — 2

3. 37 + 45 = ?

37 + 50 = ___81___

_____ − _____ = _____

So, 37 + 45 = ___82___.

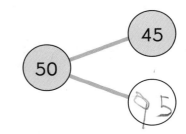

50 — 45
   — 5

4. 46 + 34 = ?

46 + 40 = ___86___

_____ − _____ = _____

So, 46 + 34 = ___86___.

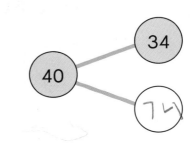

40 — 34
   — 74

Add mentally. Use number bonds to help you.

5. 41 + 43 = ___84___

6. 31 + 64 = ___95___

7. 15 + 47 = ___22___

8. 46 + 48 = ___94___

Practice 2   Mental Subtraction

Subtract mentally. First, subtract the tens. Then, subtract the ones.

─ *Example* ─

$78 - 63 = ?$

$78 - 60 =$ _____18_____

_____18_____ $-$ _____3_____ $=$ _____15_____

So, $78 - 63 =$ _____15_____.

First, subtract 60.
Then, subtract 3.

63 — 60
63 — 3

1. $89 - 57 = ?$

$89 - 50 =$ _____39_____

_____ $-$ _____ $=$ _____

So, $89 - 57 =$ _____32_____.

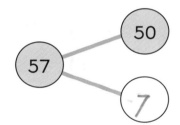

57 — 50
57 — 7

2. $75 - 33 = ?$

$75 - 30 =$ _____45_____

_____ $-$ _____ $=$ _____

So, $75 - 33 =$ _____42_____.

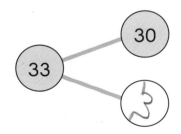

33 — 30
33 — 3

Subtract mentally.
First, subtract the tens. Then, add the extra ones.

Example

$83 - 47 = ?$

$83 - 50 = \underline{\quad 33 \quad}$

$\underline{\quad 33 \quad} + \underline{\quad 3 \quad} = \underline{\quad 36 \quad}$

So, $83 - 47 = \underline{\quad 36 \quad}$.

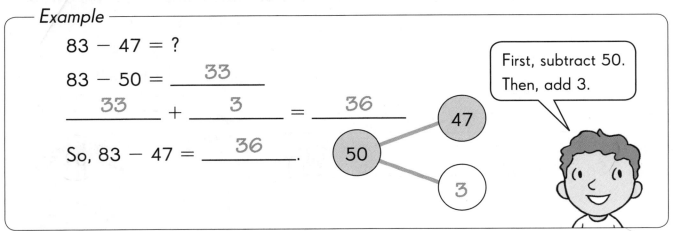

First, subtract 50.
Then, add 3.

3. $92 - 35 = ?$

$92 - 40 = \underline{\quad 22 \quad 52 \quad}$

$\underline{\qquad} + \underline{\qquad} = \underline{\qquad}$

So, $92 - 35 = \underline{\quad 22 \quad} .^5$

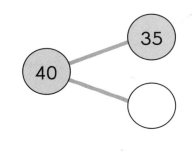

4. $87 - 18 = ?$

$87 - 20 = \underline{\quad 67 \quad}$ ✓

$\underline{\qquad} + \underline{\qquad} = \underline{\qquad}$

So, $87 - 18 = \underline{\quad 69 \quad}$.

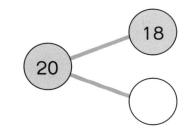

5. $72 - 44 = ?$

$72 - 50 = \underline{22}$

$\underline{} + \underline{} = \underline{}$

So, $72 - 44 = \underline{28}$.

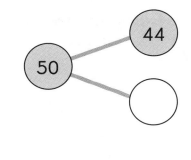

$\begin{array}{r} \overset{6}{\cancel{7}}\,12 \\ -\ 4\ 4 \\ \hline 2\ 8 \end{array}$

6. $88 - 39 = ?$

$88 - 40 = \underline{}$

$\underline{} + \underline{} = \underline{}$

So, $88 - 39 = \underline{}$.

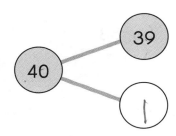

Subtract mentally. Use number bonds to help you.

7. $84 - 23 = \underline{}$ **8.** $55 - 31 = \underline{}$

9. $58 - 42 = \underline{}$ **10.** $79 - 65 = \underline{}$

11. $92 - 34 = \underline{}$ **12.** $75 - 47 = \underline{}$

13. $61 - 26 = \underline{}$ **14.** $82 - 33 = \underline{}$

15. $93 - 48 = \underline{}$ **16.** $81 - 45 = \underline{}$

$0 \times 2 = 0 \qquad 2 \times 6 = 12$
$1 \times 2 = 2 \qquad 2 \times 7 = 14$
$2 \times 2 = 4 \qquad 2 \times 8 = 16$
$2 \times 3 = 6 \qquad 2 \times 9 = 18$
$2 \times 4 = 8 \qquad 2 \times 10 = 20$
$2 \times 5 = 10$

Complete the puzzle. Use mental math.

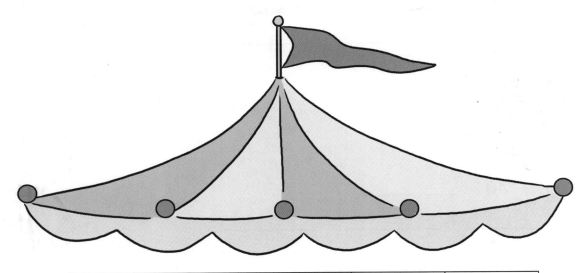

97	−	42	=	
−				
36	−	28	=	
=		−		
	−	19	=	
		=		−
				25
				=

Practice 3   More Mental Addition

Add mentally. First, add 100. Then, subtra

Add me
First, a
Ex

Then,

─ Example ─

$19 + 98 = ?$

$19 + 100 = \underline{\quad 119 \quad}$

$\underline{\quad 119 \quad} - \underline{\quad 2 \quad} = \underline{\quad 117 \quad}$

So, $19 + 98 = \underline{\quad 117 \quad}$.

1. $26 + 96 = ?$

$26 + 100 = \underline{\qquad\qquad}$

$\underline{\qquad\qquad} - \underline{\qquad\qquad} = \underline{\qquad\qquad}$

So, $26 + 96 = \underline{\qquad\qquad}$.

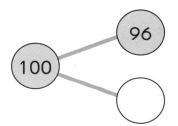

2. $38 + 95 = ?$

$38 + 100 = \underline{\qquad\qquad}$

$\underline{\qquad\qquad} - \underline{\qquad\qquad} = \underline{\qquad\qquad}$

So, $38 + 95 = \underline{\qquad\qquad}$.

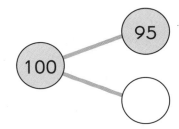

...tally.

...d the hundreds. Then, subtract the extra ones.

ample

$91 + 99 = ?$

$100 + 100 = \underline{200}$

$91 + 99 = \underline{200} - \underline{9} - \underline{1}$

$ = \underline{190}$

So, $91 + 99 = \underline{190}$.

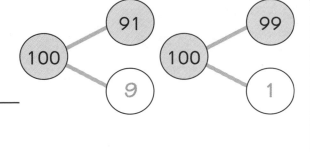

3. $98 + 96 = ?$

$100 + 100 = \underline{}$

$98 + 96 = \underline{} - \underline{} - \underline{}$

$ = \underline{}$

So, $98 + 96 = \underline{}$.

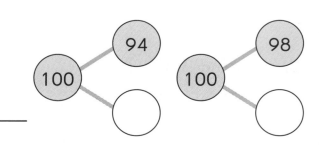

4. $94 + 98 = ?$

$100 + 100 = \underline{}$

$94 + 98 = \underline{} - \underline{} - \underline{}$

$ = \underline{}$

So, $94 + 98 = \underline{}$.

Practice 4 Rounding Numbers to Estimate

Mark (X) each number on the number line.

Number	Number line
Example 450	400 ——————— X ——————— 500
1. 330	300 ——————— 400
2. 185	100 ——————— 200
3. 2,204	2,200 ——————— 2,300

Fill in the blanks.

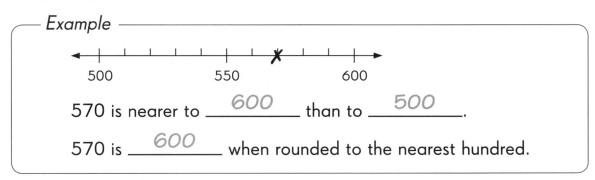

Example

500 —————— 550 ——— X —— 600

570 is nearer to ___*600*___ than to ___*500*___.

570 is ___*600*___ when rounded to the nearest hundred.

4.

800 ——— X ——— 850 ——————— 900

845 is nearer to _____ than to _____.

845 is _____ when rounded to the nearest hundred.

5.

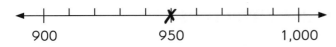

950 is nearer to _____ than to _____.

950 is _____ when rounded to the nearest hundred.

Decide whether to find an estimate or an exact answer. Solve.

> ── *Example* ───────────────────────────────
>
> An organization has about 600 members.
>
> The greatest possible number of members this can be is ___ *649* ___.
>
> The least possible number of members could be ___ *550* ___.

6. Tanya had $900. After buying two of these items, she has $210 left.

a. How much do the two items cost?

b. Which two items does she buy?

Find the sum or difference. Use rounding to check that each answer is reasonable.

┌─ *Example* ───┐

$763 + 136 =$ ___*899*___.

763 is about ___*800*___.

136 is about ___*100*___.

___*800*___ $+$ ___*100*___ $=$ ___*900*___.

So, $763 + 136$ is about ___*900*___.

___*899*___ is close to ___*900*___, so the answer is reasonable.

└───┘

7. $238 + 598 =$ _____.

238 is about _____.

598 is about _____.

_____ $+$ _____ $=$ _____.

So, $238 + 598$ is about _____.

_____ is close to _____, so the answer is reasonable.

8. $846 - 694 =$ _____.

846 is about _____.

694 is about _____.

_____ $-$ _____ $=$ _____

So, $846 - 694$ is about _____.

_____ is close to _____, so the answer is reasonable.

9.   872 − 259 = _____.

872 is about _____.

259 is about _____.

_____ − _____ = _____

So, 872 − 259 is about _____.

_____ is close to _____, so the answer is reasonable.

10.   Mrs. Ramsey wants to buy these four items.

$96 $215 $247 $385

a.   Find the total cost of the items.
Then, use rounding to check that the total cost is reasonable.

b.   Mrs. Ramsey has $980. Does she have enough money to buy all the items?

Practice 5   Using Front-End Estimation

Write the leading digit.

1.   473 _____

2.   801 _____

3.   198 _____

4.   5,147 _____

5.   7,061 _____

6.   9,625 _____

Find the sum. Use front-end estimation to check that each answer is reasonable.

Example

Find 324 + 219.

324 + 219 = __543__

324   +   219

↓   ↓

__300__ + __200__ = __500__

The estimated sum is __500__.

The answer __543__ is reasonable.

7.   Find 312 + 526.

312 + 526 = _____

312   +   526

↓   ↓

_____ + _____ = _____

The estimated sum is _____.

The answer _____ is reasonable.

Find the sum. Use front-end estimation to check that each answer is reasonable.

8. Find 364 + 509.

364 + 509 = _____

364　　+　　509

↓　　　　　　↓

_____ + _____ = _____

The estimated sum is _____.

The answer _____ is reasonable.

9. Find 286 + 473.

286 + 473 = _____

286　　+　　473

↓　　　　　　↓

_____ + _____ = _____

The estimated sum is _____.

The answer _____ is reasonable.

Find the difference. Use front-end estimation to check that each answer is reasonable.

┌─ *Example* ─────────────────────────────

Find 349 − 126.

349 − 126 = __*223*__

349　　−　　126

↓　　　　　　↓

__*300*__ − __*100*__ = __*200*__

The estimated difference is __*200*__.

The answer __*223*__ is reasonable.

└──

10. Find $618 - 372$.

$618 - 372 =$ _____

$$618 \qquad - \qquad 372$$
$$\downarrow \qquad\qquad\qquad \downarrow$$

_____ $-$ _____ $=$ _____

The estimated difference is _____.

The answer _____ is reasonable.

11. Find $936 - 528$.

$936 - 528 =$ _____

$$936 \qquad - \qquad 528$$
$$\downarrow \qquad\qquad\qquad \downarrow$$

_____ $-$ _____ $=$ _____

The estimated difference is _____.

The answer _____ is reasonable.

12. Find $759 - 236$.

$759 - 236 =$ _____

$$759 \qquad - \qquad 236$$
$$\downarrow \qquad\qquad\qquad \downarrow$$

_____ $-$ _____ $=$ _____

The estimated difference is _____.

The answer _____ is reasonable.

Solve.

13. The length of a train engine is 439 centimeters.
The length of the carriage is about 558 centimeters.
Estimate the total length of the train and the carriage.

14. A wooden pole is 356 centimeters long.
104 centimeters of it is driven into the ground.
About what height of the wooden pole is above the ground?

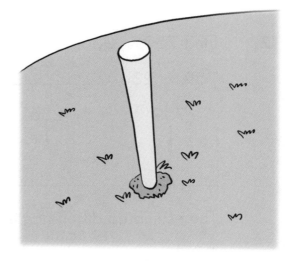

Math Journal

Fill in the blanks that show the steps to add or subtract mentally. You may use the numbers more than once.

1.   35 + 48 = ?

> **Step 1**   Add _____ to _____.
>
> _____ + _____ = _____
>
> **Step 2**   Subtract _____ from _____.
>
> _____ − _____ = _____

So, 35 + 48 = _____.

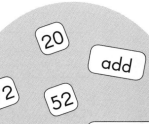

subtract
50   83
35
85   2
add

2.   72 − 18 = ?

> **Step 1**   Subtract _____ from _____.
>
> _____ − _____ = _____
>
> **Step 2**   Add _____ to _____.
>
> _____ + _____ = _____

So, 72 − 18 = _____.

20
add
72   52
subtract
54
2

Complete.

3. Explain how to round 458 to the nearest hundred.
Include a number line in your explanation.

4. Use front-end estimation to estimate the difference.
Write the steps to your solution and check that your
answer is reasonable.

905 − 178

_____

_____

_____

_____

_____

5. John used front-end estimation to estimate the sum
of 317 + 268.
Do you agree with his answer? Explain.

317 + 268 = 585

So, 317 + 268 is about 600.

_____

_____

© 2018 Marshall Cavendish Education Pte Ltd

Put On Your Thinking Cap!

Challenging Practice

1. Two numbers are rounded to the nearest hundred, then added.
The estimated sum is 500.
One number is 235. What is the greatest possible value of the other number?

2. I am a 3-digit number.
When you round me to the nearest ten and to the nearest hundred, the answer is the same.
What number can I be?

> There are many possible answers.

Put On Your Thinking Cap!

Problem Solving

Mrs. Avilla makes curtains.
She needs 356 centimeters of fabric for the kitchen
and 517 centimeters for the living room.

1. Estimate the length of the fabric she needs in all by rounding
to the nearest hundred.

2. If she buys the length of fabric estimated in Exercise 1, how
much fabric will be left over?

Cumulative Review

for Chapters 1 and 2

Concepts and Skills

Write in word form. *(Lesson 1.1)*

1. 9,999 _____

2. 1,047 _____

3. 6,005 _____

Write in standard form. *(Lesson 1.1)*

4. two thousand, twelve   _____

5. nine thousand, one   _____

6. six thousand, four hundred twenty-one   _____

Complete each number pattern. *(Lesson 1.1)*

7. 5,216 6,216 7,216 _____ _____

8. _____ _____ 3,209 3,309 3,409

9. 6,029 6,019 6,009 _____ _____

10. _____ _____ 4,021 6,021 8,021

Write the value of each digit. (Lesson 1.2)

11.

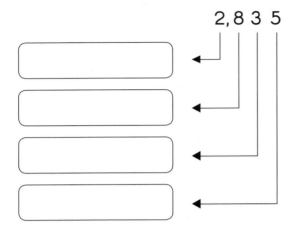

2,8 3 5

Fill in the missing numbers. (Lesson 1.2)

12. $4{,}532 = 4{,}000 +$ _____ $+ 30 + 2$

13. $1{,}000 +$ _____ $+$ _____ $= 1{,}045$

Circle the greatest number.
Underline the number that is least. (Lesson 1.3)

14.   6,329   1,987   2,456   9,000

15.   7028   7,218   7,900   7,803

Write the missing numbers. (Lesson 1.3)

16.   5,000 less than 9,702 is _____.

17.   8 more than 6,580 is _____.

18.   300 more than 6,586 is _____.

Name: _____ **Date:** _____

Order the answers in Exercise 16-18 from least to greatest. *(Lesson 1.3)*

19. _____ _____ _____

   least

Fill in the blanks. Use the digits below. *(Lesson 1.3)*

1   4   7   6

20. Form the greatest four-digit number. _____

21. Form the least four-digit number. _____

22. Form a number greater than 3,984 but less than 4,170. _____

23. Form a number greater than 6,780 but less than 7,148. _____

Find the sum or difference mentally. *(Lessons 2.1, 2.2 and 2.3)*

24. $37 + 52 =$ _____   **25.** $25 + 49 =$ _____

26. $35 + 47 =$ _____   **27.** $62 - 21 =$ _____

28. $52 - 46 =$ _____   **29.** $65 - 48 =$ _____

30. $33 + 98 =$ _____   **31.** $95 + 97 =$ _____

Round each number to the nearest hundred. *(Lesson 2.4)*

32. 852 _____   **33.** 7,592 _____

34. 3,015 _____   **35.** 1,994 _____

Find the sum or difference. Then use rounding to check that each answer is reasonable. *(Lesson 2.4)*

36. $452 + 198 =$ _____

452 rounded to the nearest hundred is _____.

198 rounded to the nearest hundred is _____.

_____ + _____ = _____

_____ is close to _____ so the answer is reasonable.

37. $909 - 493 =$ _____

909 rounded to the nearest hundred is _____.

493 rounded to the nearest hundred is _____.

_____ − _____ = _____

_____ is close to _____ so the answer is reasonable.

Find the greatest and least numbers when rounded to the nearest hundred. *(Lesson 2.4)*

38. An elevator carried about 900 kilograms. The greatest mass this can be is _____ kilograms. The least mass this can be is _____ kilograms.

Write the leading digit. *(Lesson 2.5)*

39. 2,561 _____ **40.** 897 _____

41. 5,286 _____ **42.** 9,643 _____

Find the sum or difference. Then use front-end estimation to check that each answer is reasonable. *(Lesson 2.5)*

43. 273 + 508 = _____

The estimated sum is _____.

The answer _____ is reasonable.

44. 792 − 582 = _____

The estimated difference is _____.

The answer _____ is reasonable.

Decide whether to find an estimate or an exact answer. Solve.

(Lessons 2.4, and 2.5)

45. An empty float at a parade is 125 centimeters tall.
It is fixed with 264-centimeter high decorations.
About how tall is the decorated float?

Write the missing number. *(Lesson 1.2)*

46.
- This number has four digits.
- The value of the digit in the thousands place is 1,000.
- The digit in the hundreds place is the greatest one digit number.
- The value of the digit in the tens place is 20.
- The digit in the ones place is 0.

The number is _____.

Solve.

47. A ship can carry 891 passengers.
A boat can carry 278 passengers.
Find how many more passengers the ship can carry than the boat.
Then use front-end estimation to check that your answer is reasonable.

The ship can carry _____ more passengers than the boat.

_____ is close to _____, so the answer is reasonable.

48. A school has 293 girls. It has 108 more boys than girls.
Find the total number of students in the school.
Then use rounding to check that your answer is reasonable.
Round each given number to the nearest 100.

The school has _____ students.

_____ is close to _____ so the answer is reasonable.

Chapter 3 Addition up to 10,000

Practice 1   Addition Without Regrouping

Add.

Example

```
   2,508
+    491
  -------
   2,999
```

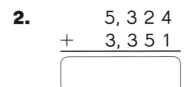

Remember:

Step 1	Add the ones.
Step 2	Add the tens.
Step 3	Add the hundreds.
Step 4	Add the thousands.

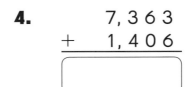

1.
```
   6,210
+    765
  -------
```

2.
```
   5,324
+  3,351
  -------
```

3.
```
   5,413
+  1,382
  -------
```

4.
```
   7,363
+  1,406
  -------
```

5.
```
   1,048
+  3,430
  -------
```

6.
```
   3,157
+  2,242
  -------
```

Add.

Example

$1{,}854 + 120 = \underline{\quad 1{,}974 \quad}$

$$
\begin{array}{r}
1{,}854 \\
+\quad 120 \\
\hline
\boxed{1{,}974}
\end{array}
$$

---

7. $5{,}362 + 506 =$ _____

8. $6{,}542 + 3{,}050 =$ _____

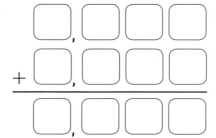

9. $4{,}632 + 5{,}306 =$ _____

10. $741 + 2{,}100 =$ _____

Find the sum. Use base-ten blocks to help you.

> **Example**
>
> The sum of 6,324 and 251 is __*6,575*__.

11.   The sum of 8,624 and 1,362 is _____.

12.   The sum of 3,452 and 5,037 is _____.

Add.

> **Example**
>
> $2,516 + 3 = $ __*2,519*__ (e)

13. $3,005 + 4 = $ _____ (o)

14. $6,015 + 24 = $ _____ (t)

15. $2,021 + 42 = $ _____ (f)

16. $8,600 + 300 = $ _____ (r)

17. $2,362 + 606 = $ _____ (o)

18. $3,633 + 1,143 = $ _____ (n)

19. $4,361 + 3,015 = $ _____ (d)

Write the matching letters of each answer to find out what "Buenas tardes" means.

20.   It means G _____ _____ _____
                          2,968 3,009 7,376

A _____ _____ *e* _____ _____ _____ _____ _____.
  2,063 6,039 2,519 8,900 4,776 2,968 3,009 4,776

Add. Show your work.

Example

3,132 + 624 = _3,756_

Work

$$
\begin{array}{r}
3,1\ 3\ 2 \\
+\quad\ 6\ 2\ 4 \\
\hline
3,7\ 5\ 6 \\
\end{array}
$$

21. 4,094 + 803 = _____

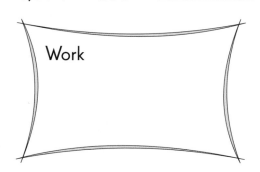

Work

22. 5,051 + 2,136 = _____

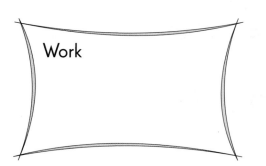

Work

23. 7,423 + 1,362 = _____

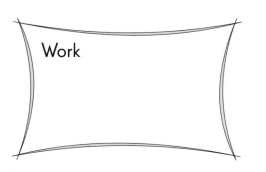

Work

24. 6,036 + 3,112 = _____

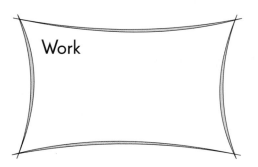

Work

25. 8,999 + 1,000 = _____

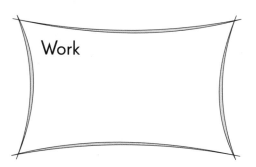

Work

Practice 2   Addition with Regrouping in Hundreds

Add. Use base-ten blocks to help you.

Example

$$\begin{array}{r} \overset{1}{5},3\,0\,0 \\ +\ 2\,,8\,0\,0 \\ \hline 8{,}1\,0\,0 \end{array}$$

1.
$$\begin{array}{r} 3\,,8\,0\,0 \\ +\ 1\,,6\,0\,0 \\ \hline \end{array}$$

2.
$$\begin{array}{r} 1\,,5\,0\,0 \\ +\ \ \ \ 9\,0\,0 \\ \hline \end{array}$$

3.
$$\begin{array}{r} 3\,,8\,0\,0 \\ +\ 2\,,8\,0\,0 \\ \hline \end{array}$$

4.
$$\begin{array}{r} 3\,,7\,0\,0 \\ +\ 2\,,5\,0\,0 \\ \hline \end{array}$$

5.
$$\begin{array}{r} 2\,,6\,0\,0 \\ +\ 1\,,4\,0\,0 \\ \hline \end{array}$$

6.
$$\begin{array}{r} 1\,,1\,0\,0 \\ +\ 1\,,9\,0\,0 \\ \hline \end{array}$$

7.
$$\begin{array}{r} 4\,,9\,0\,0 \\ +\ 3\,,3\,0\,0 \\ \hline \end{array}$$

8.
$$\begin{array}{r} 4\,,8\,0\,0 \\ +\ 2\,,3\,0\,0 \\ \hline \end{array}$$

9.
$$\begin{array}{r} 7\,,6\,0\,0 \\ +\ 1\,,7\,0\,0 \\ \hline \end{array}$$

Add. Show your work.

Example

$1{,}730 + 2{,}604 =$ ___4,334___

Work

$$\begin{array}{r} 1{,}730 \\ +\ 2{,}604 \\ \hline 4{,}334 \end{array}$$

10. $3{,}876 + 2{,}821 =$ _____

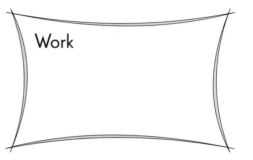

Work

11. $3{,}610 + 1{,}927 =$ _____

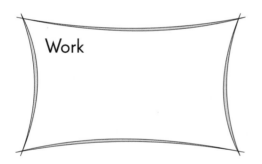

Work

12. $1{,}900 + 5{,}511 =$ _____

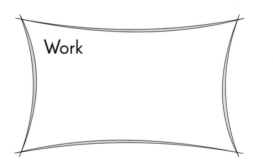

Work

13. $5{,}516 + 2{,}883 =$ _____

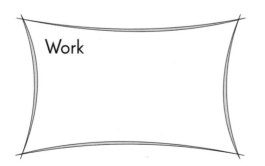

Work

14. $6{,}325 + 2{,}802 =$ _____

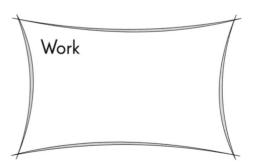

Work

Practice 3   Addition with Regrouping in Ones, Tens, and Hundreds

Follow the steps to add. Fill in the blanks.

1.

Step 1

$$\begin{array}{r} {}^{1}\\ 5,5\,3\,2 \\ +\ \ 2,9\,8\,9 \\ \hline \end{array}$$

Add the ones and regroup the ones.

2 ones + 9 ones

= _____ ones

= _____ ten _____ one

Step 2

$$\begin{array}{r} {}^{1\ 1}\\ 5,5\,3\,2 \\ +\ \ 2,9\,8\,9 \\ \hline \end{array}$$

Add the tens and regroup the tens.

1 ten + 3 tens + 8 tens

= _____ tens

= _____ hundred _____ tens

Step 3

$$\begin{array}{r} {}^{1\ 1\ 1}\\ 5,5\,3\,2 \\ +\ \ 2,9\,8\,9 \\ \hline \end{array}$$

Add the hundreds and regroup the hundreds.

1 hundred + 5 hundreds + 9 hundreds

= _____ hundreds

= _____ thousand _____ hundreds

Step 4

$$\begin{array}{r} {}^{1\ 1\ 1}\\ 5,5\,3\,2 \\ +\ \ 2,9\,8\,9 \\ \hline \end{array}$$

Add the thousands.

1 thousand + 5 thousands + 2 thousands

= _____ thousands

Add.

Example

$$\begin{array}{r}{}^{1\ 1\ 1}\\ 8\ 9\ 7\\ +\quad 9\ 2\ 4\\ \hline 1,8\ 2\ 1\end{array}$$

2.
$$\begin{array}{r}2\ 1\ 5\\ +\quad 7\ 9\ 6\\ \hline \end{array}$$

3.
$$\begin{array}{r}1,0\ 6\ 3\\ +\quad 4\ 2\ 9\\ \hline \end{array}$$

4.
$$\begin{array}{r}1,1\ 9\ 8\\ +\quad 6\ 2\ 2\\ \hline \end{array}$$

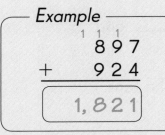

5.
$$\begin{array}{r}3,3\ 2\ 9\\ +\ 1,5\ 9\ 7\\ \hline \end{array}$$

6.
$$\begin{array}{r}6,2\ 5\ 8\\ +\ 2,9\ 3\ 7\\ \hline \end{array}$$

7.
$$\begin{array}{r}1,4\ 0\ 6\\ +\quad 8\ 6\\ \hline \end{array}$$

8.
$$\begin{array}{r}3,6\ 7\ 4\\ +\ 1,6\ 6\ 7\\ \hline \end{array}$$

9.
$$\begin{array}{r}6\ 5\ 7\\ +\quad 9\ 4\ 3\\ \hline \end{array}$$

10.
$$\begin{array}{r}6,4\ 3\ 5\\ +\ 2,6\ 8\ 9\\ \hline \end{array}$$

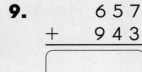

Fill in the blank.

11. Christopher Columbus landed on an island in the Caribbean in _____.
(Hint: The value appears twice on this page.)

Solve.

Example

A baker makes 3,452 bagels in the morning.
He makes another 759 bagels in the afternoon.
How many bagels does he make in all?

3,452 + 759 = 4,211

The baker makes ____4,211____ bagels in all.

---

12. A grocer sells 6,835 apples and 2,795 oranges.
How many pieces of fruit does she sell in all?

She sells _____ pieces of fruit in all.

Solve.

13. Molly's bakery sells 5,268 muffins.
Then Molly has 1,952 muffins left.
How many muffins does she have at first?

Molly has _____ muffins at first.

14. Mr. Sanchez has 2,156 gold coins and 3,152 silver coins.
How many coins does he have in all?

Mr. Sanchez has _____ coins in all.

Put On Your Thinking Cap!

 Challenging Practice

**Use the digits below. Make as many 4-digit numbers as you can.
Do not begin with '0'.
For each number, use each digit only once.
Then add two 4-digit numbers where you do not need to regroup.**

3   5   9   2   0   7

1.

Now you try it!

```
    5, 2 0 7
 +  3, 0 7 2
 ──────────
    8, 2 7 9
```

Use the digits below. Make as many 4-digit numbers as you can.
Do not begin with '0'.
For each number, use each digit only once.
Then add two 4-digit numbers where you need to regroup.

4   8   1   0   6   9

$$
\begin{array}{r}
{}^{1}\;{}^{1}\;\;\;\\
1,648 \\
+\;\;6,980 \\
\hline
8,628
\end{array}
$$

2.

Now you try it!

Put On Your Thinking Cap!

 Problem Solving

Find the missing numbers.

1.
```
  3, 6  2  5
+ 2, 2 [ ] 4
_____
  5, 8  8  9
```

2.
```
  2, [ ] 8  8
+ 3,  6  1  5
_____
  6,  1  0  3
```

Find the page numbers of the book.

3.

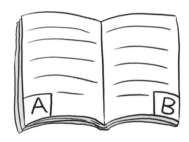

Each of the pages has a 3-digit page number.
The number on Page A is an even number.
The sum of its digits is 7.
The number on Page B is an odd number.
The sum of its digits is 8.
What are the two possible page numbers for
Page A and Page B?

Page 123:
Sum of digits
= 1 + 2 + 3
= 6

Solve.

4. Find two numbers whose sum is 100.

   _____ ◯ _____ = 100

5. Find three numbers whose sum is 150.

   _____ ◯ _____ ◯ _____ = 150

6. A student has four digits.

   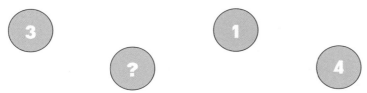

   The digit in ⬤? is greater than each of the other digits but is less than the sum of these digits.

   What is the greatest possible digit?

Use the given digits and the answer you found in Exercise 6 to answer Exercises 7 to 9.

7. What is the greatest possible 4-digit number?

8. What is the least possible 4-digit number?

9. What is the sum of the 4-digit numbers in Exercises 7 and 8?

Subtraction up to 10,000

Practice 1   Subtraction Without Regrouping

Subtract.

Example

$$
\begin{array}{r}
3,817 \\
-\ \ \ 705 \\
\hline
3,112
\end{array}
$$

1.
$$
\begin{array}{r}
9,349 \\
-\ 5,138 \\
\hline
\end{array}
$$

2.
$$
\begin{array}{r}
7,352 \\
-\ 4,321 \\
\hline
\end{array}
$$

Subtract. Use base-ten blocks to help you.

Example

$$5,286 - 5,123 = \underline{\ 163\ }$$

3. $3,646 - 2,523 = \underline{\hspace{2cm}}$

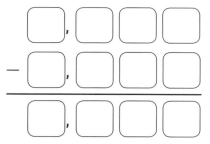

4. $9,646 - 523 = \underline{\hspace{2cm}}$

5. $5,564 - 23 = \underline{\hspace{2cm}}$

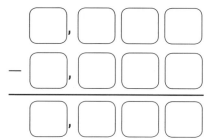

Find the difference. Use base-ten blocks to help you.

> **Example**
>
> The difference between 7,249 and 249 is ___7,000___.

6. The difference between 5,286 and 5,000 is _____.

7. The difference between 4,301 and 2,101 is _____.

Subtract.

> **Example**
>
> $3,497 - 2,391 =$ ___1,106___
>
> Work
> ```
>    3, 4 9 7
> −  2, 3 9 1
> ───────────
>    1, 1 0 6
> ```

8. $8,421 - 310 =$ _____

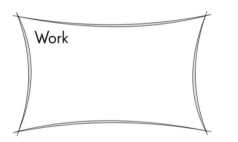

Work

9. $9,786 - 72 =$ _____

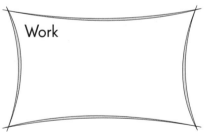

Work

10. $6,974 - 1,813 =$ _____

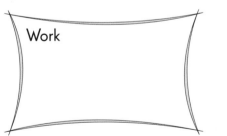

Work

11. $7,568 - 4,022 =$ _____

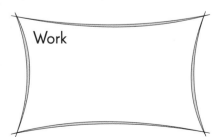

Work

12. $5,493 - 3,291 =$ _____

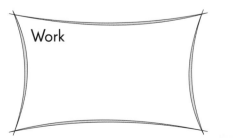

Work

© 2018 Marshall Cavendish Education Pte Ltd

Practice 2 Subtraction with Regrouping in Hundreds and Thousands

Subtract.

┌─ *Example* ──────────────┐
│   │
│   ⁵ ₆ ¹ 0 0 0   │
│   −   8 0 0   │
│   ──────────────   │
│   5, 2 0 0   │
│   │
└──────────────────────────┘

1.   3, 6 0 0
       − 1, 7 0 0
       ──────────

2.   2, 6 5 9
       − 1, 9 4 3
       ──────────

3.   6, 4 9 1
       − 3, 5 7 0
       ──────────

4.   5, 0 6 4
       − 4, 7 3 2
       ──────────

5.   9, 2 5 6
       − 3, 6 2 5
       ──────────

Subtract. Show your work.

┌─ *Example* ──────────────┐
│   │
│   8,175 − 3,602   │
│   = ____4,573____   │
│   │
│   ⁷ ₈ ¹ 1 7 5   │
│   −   3, 6 0 2   │
│   ──────────   │
│   4, 5 7 3   │
│   │
└──────────────────────────┘

6. 9,356 − 7,841

= _____

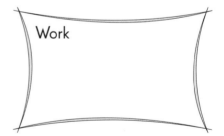
Work

7. 2,394 − 1,650

= _____

Work

8. 3,084 − 1,601

= _____

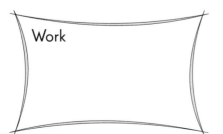
Work

9. 7,079 − 653

= _____

Work

10. 9,087 − 904

= _____

Work

Subtract and solve.

Example

$8,500 - 700 = \underline{7,800}$ – · – –

11. $2,600 - 900 = \underline{\hspace{2cm}}$ · –

12. $5,120 - 600 = \underline{\hspace{2cm}}$ – – –

13. $4,789 - 1,800 = \underline{\hspace{2cm}}$ ·

14. $9,363 - 5,512 = \underline{\hspace{2cm}}$ – – ·

15. $3,255 - 1,731 = \underline{\hspace{2cm}}$ – ·

16. $3,126 - 1,724 = \underline{\hspace{2cm}}$ –

17. $6,043 - 3,712 = \underline{\hspace{2cm}}$ · · –

Find the secret message. Match each answer and its symbol to the letters in the table.

A	B	C	D	E	F	G	H	I
·–	–··	–·–	–··	·	··–·	––·	····	··

J	K	L	M	N	O	P	Q	R
·–––	–·–	·–··	––	–··	–––	·––·	––·–	–·

S	T	U	V	W	X	Y	Z	
···	–	··–	···–	·––	–··–	–·––	––··	

Fill in each blank.

18. " $\underset{7,800}{\text{Y}}$ $\underset{4,520}{\underline{\hspace{1cm}}}$ $\underset{2,331}{\underline{\hspace{1cm}}}$, $\underset{1,524}{\underline{\hspace{1cm}}}$ $\underset{2,989}{\underline{\hspace{1cm}}}$

$\underset{3,851}{\underline{\hspace{1cm}}}$ $\underset{1,524}{\underline{\hspace{1cm}}}$ $\underset{2,989}{\underline{\hspace{1cm}}}$ $\underset{1,700}{\underline{\hspace{1cm}}}$ $\underset{1,402}{\underline{\hspace{1cm}}}$!"

Practice 3   Subtraction with Regrouping in Ones, Tens, Hundreds, and Thousands

Subtract. Fill in the blanks.

1.

```
┌─ Example ──────────────────────────────────────────────────┐
│                          6                                  │
│   Step 1      8, 2 X̶ ¹0      Subtract the ones.             │
│             − 1, 3 7 9       9 ones cannot be subtracted    │
│             ───────────      from 0 ones.                   │
│                       1      So, regroup the tens and ones. │
│                                                             │
│                              7 tens 0 ones                  │
│                                                             │
│                              = _____ tens _____ ones │
└─────────────────────────────────────────────────────────────┘
```

Step 2   8, 2 7 0   Subtract the tens.
          − 1, 3 7 9   7 tens cannot be subtracted from 6 tens.
          ───────────   So, regroup the hundreds and tens.

2 hundreds 6 tens

= _____ hundred _____ tens

Step 3   8, 2 7 0   Subtract the hundreds.
          − 1, 3 7 9   3 hundreds cannot be subtracted from

_____ hundred.
So, regroup the thousands and hundreds.

8 thousands 1 hundred

= _____ thousands _____ hundreds

Step 4   8, 2 7 0   Subtract the thousands.
          − 1, 3 7 9

Subtract. Fill in the blanks.

2.

Step 1	$4,3\overset{4}{\cancel{5}}\overset{1}{7}$ $-\ 1,7\ 8\ 9$	Subtract the ones. 9 ones cannot be subtracted from 7 ones. So, regroup the tens and ones. 5 tens 7 ones = _____ tens _____ ones

Step 2	$4,\overset{2}{\cancel{3}}\overset{1}{\cancel{5}}\overset{1}{7}$ $-\ 1,7\ 8\ 9$	Subtract the tens. 8 tens cannot be subtracted from _____ tens. So, regroup the hundreds and tens. 3 hundreds 4 tens = _____ hundreds _____ tens

Step 3	$\overset{3}{\cancel{4}},\overset{1}{\overset{2}{\cancel{3}}}\overset{1}{\overset{4}{\cancel{5}}}\overset{1}{7}$ $-\ 1,7\ 8\ 9$	Subtract the hundreds. 7 hundreds cannot be subtracted from _____ hundreds. So, regroup the thousands and hundreds. 4 thousands 2 hundreds. = _____ thousands _____ hundreds

Step 4	$\overset{3}{\cancel{4}},\overset{1}{\overset{2}{\cancel{3}}}\overset{1}{\overset{4}{\cancel{5}}}\overset{1}{7}$ $-\ 1,7\ 8\ 9$	Subtract the thousands.

Subtract. Regroup when needed.

3.
```
    8 9 3
  − 5 8 4
```

4.
```
    5 5 6
  − 2 8 7
```

5.
```
  1, 4 3 6
  −   3 8 8
```

6.
```
  2, 1 1 1
  −   1 9 7
```

7.
```
  9, 1 9 1
  − 2, 5 6 3
```

8.
```
    7 0 4
  −   2 9
```

9.   **Color the answers from above to find the path to the present.**

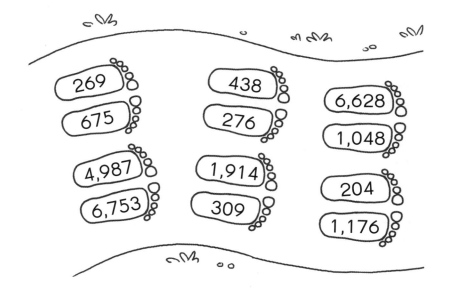

269
675
4,987
6,753
438
276
1,914
309
6,628
1,048
204
1,176

Subtract. Regroup when needed.

Example

$3{,}852 - 1{,}621 = \underline{2{,}231}$ (F)

10. $7{,}162 - 5{,}002 = \underline{}$ (S)

11. $7{,}156 - 43 = \underline{}$ (A)

12. $3{,}696 - 2{,}475 = \underline{}$ (I)

13. $7{,}342 - 2{,}502 = \underline{}$ (T)

14. $8{,}513 - 566 = \underline{}$ (E)

15. $6{,}707 - 1{,}125 = \underline{}$ (L)

16. $2{,}152 - 1{,}648 = \underline{}$ (Y)

17. $5{,}261 - 85 = \underline{}$ (U)

18. $9{,}133 - 7{,}269 = \underline{}$ (R)

19. $3{,}087 - 1{,}779 = \underline{}$ (B)

20. $7{,}965 - 978 = \underline{}$ (O)

Write the corresponding letters from Exercise 11 to 20 to find the name of this national treasure.

21.

| 2,160 | 4,840 | 7,113 | 4,840 | 5,176 | 7,947 |

| | F |
| 6,987 | 2,231 |

| 5,582 | 1,221 | 1,308 | 7,947 | 1,864 | 4,840 | 504 |

22. Where is this national treasure located?

_____ _____

Practice 4   Subtraction Across Zeros

Subtract. Then solve.

Example

$$
\begin{array}{r}
{}^{0\ 9\ 9}_{\ 1\ 1\ 1}1,000 \\
-\quad 343 \\
\hline
657
\end{array}
$$

(P)

1.
$$
\begin{array}{r}
1,000 \\
-\quad 764 \\
\hline
\end{array}
$$
(y)

2.
$$
\begin{array}{r}
2,000 \\
-\quad 358 \\
\hline
\end{array}
$$
(e)

3.
$$
\begin{array}{r}
6,000 \\
-\ 1,437 \\
\hline
\end{array}
$$
(t)

4.
$$
\begin{array}{r}
3,000 \\
-\ 2,515 \\
\hline
\end{array}
$$
(r)

5.
$$
\begin{array}{r}
4,000 \\
-\ 1,637 \\
\hline
\end{array}
$$
(a)

6.
$$
\begin{array}{r}
8,004 \\
-\ 5,476 \\
\hline
\end{array}
$$
(w)

7.
$$
\begin{array}{r}
9,001 \\
-\ 5,557 \\
\hline
\end{array}
$$
(s)

8.
$$
\begin{array}{r}
7,000 \\
-\ 1,999 \\
\hline
\end{array}
$$
(b)

9.
$$
\begin{array}{r}
5,003 \\
-\ 2,349 \\
\hline
\end{array}
$$
(z)

Write the corresponding letters to find the flavor of the jam.

10.

____	____	____	____	____	____	____	____	____	____
3,444	4,563	485	2,363	2,528	5,001	1,642	485	485	236

Solve. Show your work.

Example

Sarah has 1,000 stickers.
Maria has 450 stickers.
How many more stickers does Sarah have than Maria?

$$
\begin{array}{r}
\overset{9}{\cancel{1,0}}{}^{10}0\ 0 \\
-\quad\ \ 4\ 5\ 0 \\
\hline
5\ 5\ 0
\end{array}
$$

Sarah has _____ more stickers than Maria.

---

11. Pete wants to deliver 4,002 oranges to a retirement home.
He has 2,157 oranges.
How many more oranges does he need?

Pete needs _____ more oranges.

Put On Your Thinking Cap!

Challenging Practice

Fill in the blanks in each number sentence.
Use the numbers in the box.

1. The difference between two numbers is 42.

| 68 | 42 | 26 | 82 |

☐ − ☐ = ☐

2. The difference between two numbers is 280.

| 400 | 196 | 129 | 476 | 280 |

☐ − ☐ = ☐

Fill in the missing numbers.

3.
```
  5, ☐ 3 6
− 2, 7 2 4
───────────
  2, 9 1 2
```

4.
```
  8, ☐ 7 5
− 3, 4 4 3
───────────
  4, 7 3 2
```

Fill in the missing numbers.

5.
```
    3,  6  8  9
 -  2, [ ] 9  5
 ─────────────
       9  9  4
```

6.
```
    7,  3  2 [ ]
 - [ ]  8  7  9
 ─────────────
    3,  4  4  6
```

Solve. Use the digits to make 4-digit numbers. Show your work. Do not begin any number with '0'.

```
 6   5   8   2   0
```

7. Subtract the least 4-digit number from the greatest 4-digit number.

_____ − _____ = _____

Solve.

8. Write a number greater than 5,632 using the digits 0, 1, 4, 7. Then subtract 5,632 from the number.

_____ − _____ = _____

Put On Your Thinking Cap!

Problem Solving

Solve. Show your work.

1. The difference between two numbers is 100.
One number is more than 90 but less than 100.
The other number is between 190 and 200.
What are the two possible numbers?

The two possible answers are _____ and _____.

2. Lilian went shopping with $1,000.
She saw five items on display in a shop window.
After buying two items, she had $732 left.
Which two items did she buy?

$68

$32

$25

$500

$200

She bought the _____ and _____.

Solve.

3. Nick and Isaac are at a school fair.
They want to collect points to exchange for these prizes.

pencil

| 30 Points |

notebook

| 50 Points |

crayons

| 100 Points |

pencil holder

| 200 Points |

stationery set

| 500 Points |

backpack

| 1,000 Points |

At the fair games, Nick has 215 points and Isaac has 78 points.
They combine their points to exchange for three prizes.
What are the two sets of three prizes they can get?

a. _____

b. _____

Using Bar Models: Addition and Subtraction

Practice 1   Real-World Problems: Addition and Subtraction

Solve. Use bar models to help you.

— *Example* —

A biking team raises $4,250 for charity.
A running team raises $825 more than the biking team.

a. How much money does the running team raise?

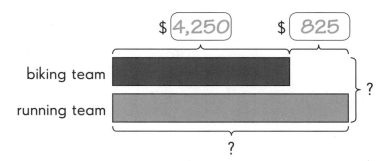

$ _4,250_ ⊕ $ _825_ = $ _5,075_

The running team raises $ _5,075_ .

b. How much money do both teams raise in all?

$ _4,250_ ⊕ $ _5,075_ = $ _9,325_

Both teams raise $ _9,325_ in all.

Solve. Use bar models to help you.

1. The third graders collect 487 cans of food for a food drive.
    The second graders collect 175 fewer cans than the third graders.
    a. How many cans do the second graders collect?

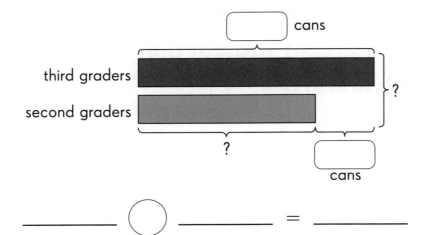

    The second graders collect _____ cans.

    b. How many cans do both grades collect in all?

    _____ ◯ _____ = _____

    Both grades collect _____ cans in all.

Name: _____   **Date:** _____

Solve. Use bar models to help you.

2. A bookshop has 4,320 books and magazines.
It has 2,169 books. The rest are magazines.

a. How many magazines does the bookshop have?

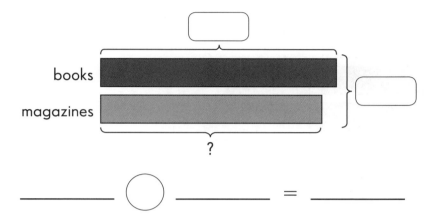

_____ ◯ _____ = _____

The bookshop has _____ magazines.

b. There are 1,493 women's magazines and the rest are
sports magazines.
How many sports magazines does the bookshop have?

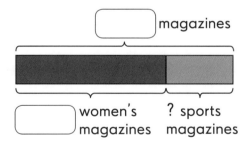

_____ ◯ _____ = _____

The bookshop has _____ sports magazines.

Solve. Use bar models to help you.

3. Ray's rope is 1,452 centimeters long.
Hannah's rope is 379 centimeters longer than Ray's rope.

a. How long is Hannah's rope?

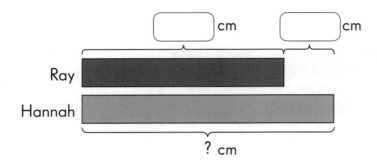

[ ] cm   [ ] cm

Ray

Hannah

? cm

_____ ◯ _____ = _____

Hannah's rope is _____ centimeters long.

b. Ray uses 645 centimeters of his rope.
How long is his remaining rope?

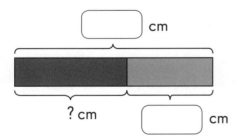

[ ] cm

? cm   [ ] cm

_____ ◯ _____ = _____

Ray's remaining rope is _____ centimeters long.

Practice 2 Real-World Problems: Addition and Subtraction

Solve. Draw bar models to help you.

Example

Janice has 1,458 stamps.
She has 396 fewer stamps than Ben.

a. How many stamps does Ben have?

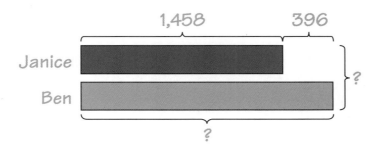

_____1,458_____ (+) _____396_____ = _____1,854_____

Ben has ___1,854___ stamps.

b. How many stamps do they have in all?

_____1,458_____ (+) _____1,854_____ = _____3,312_____

They have ___3,312___ stamps in all.

Solve. Draw bar models to help you.

1. There are 1,287 men at a baseball game.
There are 879 fewer women than men at the game.

a. How many women are at the game?

_____ women are at the game.

b. How many adult spectators are at the game?

_____ adult spectators are at the game.

Solve. Draw bar models to help you.

2.   A school sets aside $4,756 for its athletic fund.
It sets aside $1,297 less for its library fund.
a.   How much money is in the library fund?

$_____ is in the library fund.

b. $948 is spent from the library fund.
How much money is left?

$_____ is left in the library fund.

Solve. Draw bar models to help you.

3. The school clerk prints 635 newsletters on Monday.
She prints 96 fewer newsletters on Wednesday.

    a. How many newsletters does she print on Wednesday?

    b. How many newsletters does she print in all?

Solve. Draw bar models to help you.

4.   Mr. Tuzamoto's factory makes 1,793 toys each day.
It makes 157 more toys than Ms. Jefferson's factory.

    a. How many toys does Ms. Jefferson's factory make each day?

    Ms. Jefferson's factory makes _____ toys each day.

    b. If Ms. Jefferson's factory sells 698 toys, how many toys does her factory have left?

    Ms. Jefferson's factory has _____ toys left.

Solve. Draw bar models to help you.

5. A middle school has 3,756 students.
It has 455 fewer students than an elementary school.

   a. How many students does the elementary school have?

   b. How many students do both schools have in all?

Practice 3   Real-World Problems: Addition and Subtraction

Solve. Draw bar models to help you.

— *Example* —

Jake mixes 620 liters of water and
180 liters of syrup to make lemonade.
He adds another 145 liters of water to the mixture.
How much more water than syrup does he use
for the lemonade?

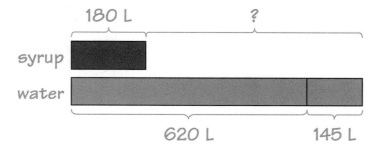

620 + 145 = 765

He uses 765 liters of water.

765 – 180 = 585

He uses 585 liters more water than syrup.

Solve. Draw bar models to help you.

1. A pet store donates 3,500 pounds of dog food to an animal shelter.
    A farm donates 2,500 pounds of dog food at first.
    Later it donates another 2,000 pounds of dog food to the animal shelter.
    How many more pounds of dog food does the farm donate than the pet store?

Math Journal

Write your own real-world problem.
Solve. Draw bar models to help you.

> The Park Fund
> raises $2,960.
> The Playground
> Fund raises $2,662.

> The Park Fund raises $298 more
> than the Playground Fund.
> The Playground Fund raises $298
> less than the Park Fund.
> The Park Fund and the Playground
> Fund raise $5,622 in all.

Example

Word problem

The Park Fund raises $2,960.
The Playground Fund raises $298 less than the Park Fund.
How much does the Playground Fund raise?

Model

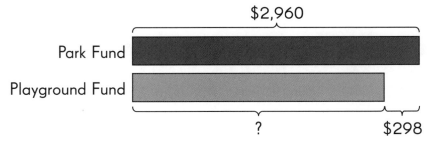

$2,960

Park Fund

Playground Fund

? $298

Solution

$2,960 − $298 = $2,662

The Playground Fund raises $2,662.

Now you try it!

Word problem

Model

Solution

Put On Your Thinking Cap!

 Challenging Practice

Look at the cards.

318	456	195
A	B	C

Think of three ways to choose two cards.
Find the sum of the two cards.

┌─ *Example* ───┐

A and B; ___318___ + ___456___ = ___774___

└──┘

1. _____ and _____ ; _____ + _____ = _____

2. _____ and _____ ; _____ + _____ = _____

Fill in the missing letters.

3. Which two cards give the greatest sum? _____ and _____

4. Which two cards give the least sum? _____ and _____

5. Which two cards give the greatest difference? _____ and _____

6. Which two cards give the least difference? _____ and _____

# Put On Your Thinking Cap!

Problem Solving

1. Carlos has been collecting cards since he was 5 years old.
He has not thrown away any of his cards.
He is now 7 years old.
He collected 201 cards last year.
He collects 125 cards this year.
He has a total of 589 cards now.

a. How many cards did he have in total at the end of last year?
b. How many cards did he collect when he was 5 years old?

2. Jason, Peter, and Ken hold a garage sale for charity.
Jason raises $350.
Peter raises $20 more than Jason.
Ken raises the same amount as the total amount raised by Jason and Peter.

How much money do the three boys raise in all?

Cumulative Review

for Chapters 3 to 5

Concepts and Skills

Add. *(Lessons 3.1, 3.2, and 3.3)*

1.
$$6,305$$
$$+\quad 2,512$$
⬚

2.
$$3,100$$
$$+\quad 2,800$$
⬚

Subtract. *(Lessons 4.1, 4.2 and 4.3)*

3.
$$8,754$$
$$-\quad\quad 531$$
⬚

4.
$$8,615$$
$$-\quad 2,704$$
⬚

Fill in the missing numbers.

5.
$$\boxed{},265$$
$$+\quad 2,058$$
$$\overline{\quad 6,323}$$

6.
$$4,672$$
$$+\quad 3,\boxed{}79$$
$$\overline{\quad 8,251}$$

7.
$$2,\boxed{}61$$
$$-\quad\quad 684$$
$$\overline{\quad 1,877}$$

8.
$$5,010$$
$$-\quad \boxed{}685$$
$$\overline{\quad 1,325}$$

Complete. *(Lesson 4.4)*

9. Gabriel and Sue are at an amusement park.
   a. Gabriel throws two darts at a target board.
   The difference between the two numbers is 75.
   Circle the two numbers.

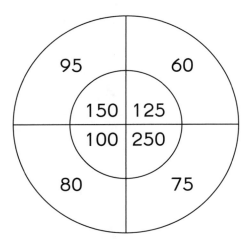

   b. Sue throws two darts at another target board.
   The difference between the two numbers is 2,700.
   Circle the two numbers.

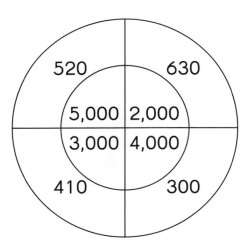

Problem Solving

Solve. Draw bar models to help you. *(Lesson 5.1)*

10. 5,476 people ride Bus D in March.
1,496 fewer people ride Bus E in the same month.
  a. How many people ride Bus E in March?
  b. How many people ride both buses in March?

11. A supermarket has 1,213 apples.
368 are green apples.
  a. How many of the apples are red?
  b. How many more red apples than green apples does the supermarket have?

12. 2,500 people visit the Children's Museum on Monday.
On Tuesday, there were 532 more people at the museum than on Monday.
What is the total number of visitors for both days?

13. Michael has 754 songs in his audio device.
He has 98 more songs than Peter.
How many songs do they have in all?

Chapter 6

Multiplication Tables of 6, 7, 8, and 9

Practice 1   Multiplication Properties

Look at each number line. Write the multiplication fact.

1.

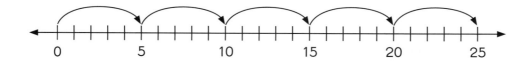

_____ × _____ = _____

2.

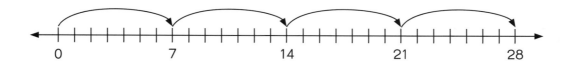

_____ × _____ = _____

3.

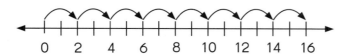

_____ × _____ = _____

Complete each multiplication fact. Then show on each number line.

4. $4 \times 5 =$ _____

5. $5 \times 3 =$ _____

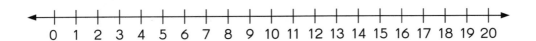

Look at the array model. Write the multiplication fact.

Example

	1	2	3	4	5
1	○	○	○	○	○
2	○	○	○	○	○

	1	2
1	○	○
2	○	○
3	○	○
4	○	○
5	○	○

___2___ × ___5___ = ___10___   ___5___ × ___2___ = ___10___

6.

	1	2	3	4
1	○	○	○	○
2	○	○	○	○
3	○	○	○	○

	1	2	3
1	○	○	○
2	○	○	○
3	○	○	○
4	○	○	○

_____ × _____ = _____   _____ × _____ = _____

© 2018 Marshall Cavendish Education Pte Ltd

Name: _____ **Date:** _____

Look at the array model. Write the multiplication fact.

7.

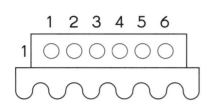

1 2 3 4 5 6

1 × _____ = _____   _____ × _____ = _____

8.

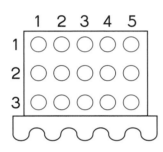

3 × _____ = _____ × 3

= _____

Complete the multiplication fact. Then show on each number line.

9.   2 × 5 = _____

5 × 2 = _____

So, _____ × 5 = 5 × _____

= _____.

Fill in the missing numbers.

10. $2 \times \underline{\hspace{2cm}} = 0 \times \underline{\hspace{2cm}}$

$= \underline{\hspace{1.5cm}}$

11. $0 \times \underline{\hspace{2cm}} = 4 \times \underline{\hspace{2cm}}$

$= \underline{\hspace{1.5cm}}$

12. $5 \times \underline{\hspace{2cm}} = 1 \times \underline{\hspace{2cm}}$

$= \underline{\hspace{1.5cm}}$

13. $1 \times \underline{\hspace{2cm}} = 10 \times \underline{\hspace{2cm}}$

$= \underline{\hspace{1.5cm}}$

Complete each multiplication fact. Then show on the number line.

Example

$2 \times 3 \times 3 = ?$

Step 1 $2 \times 3 = \underline{\hspace{1cm} 6 \hspace{1cm}}$

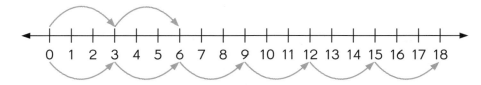

Step 2 $6 \times 3 = \underline{\hspace{1cm} 18 \hspace{1cm}}$

So, $2 \times 3 \times 3 = \underline{\hspace{1cm} 6 \hspace{1cm}} \times \underline{\hspace{1cm} 3 \hspace{1cm}}$

$= \underline{\hspace{1cm} 18 \hspace{1cm}}$

14. $2 \times 4 \times 2 = \underline{\hspace{2cm}} \times \underline{\hspace{2cm}}$

$= \underline{\hspace{1.5cm}}$

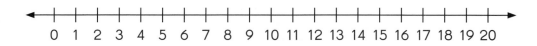

Practice 2 Multiply by 6

Look at each array model. Write the multiplication fact.

┌─ *Example* ─────────────────────────────────┐

      1 2 3 4 5 6

   1 ○ ○ ○ ○ ○ ○
   2 ○ ○ ○ ○ ○ ○
   3 ○ ○ ○ ○ ○ ○
   4 ○ ○ ○ ○ ○ ○

   ____4____ × ____6____ = ____24____

└──┘

1.

      1 2 3 4 5 6

   1 ○ ○ ○ ○ ○ ○
   2 ○ ○ ○ ○ ○ ○
   3 ○ ○ ○ ○ ○ ○
   4 ○ ○ ○ ○ ○ ○
   5 ○ ○ ○ ○ ○ ○

   _____ × _____ = _____

2.

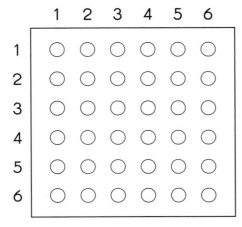

      1 2 3 4 5 6

   1 ○ ○ ○ ○ ○ ○
   2 ○ ○ ○ ○ ○ ○
   3 ○ ○ ○ ○ ○ ○
   4 ○ ○ ○ ○ ○ ○
   5 ○ ○ ○ ○ ○ ○
   6 ○ ○ ○ ○ ○ ○

   _____ × _____ = _____

Fill in the missing numbers.

3.   8 sixes = 8 × _____

4.   5 × 6 = _____ sixes

5.   7 + 7 + 7 + 7 + 7 + 7 = 6 × _____

6.   6 + 6 + 6 + 6 + 6 + 6 + 6 = 7 × _____

7.   10 × 6 = 6 × _____

8.   3 sixes = 6 + 6 + _____

Multiply. Use multiplication facts you know to find other multiplication facts.

9.   6 × 4 = _____ groups of 4

           = 5 groups of 4 + _____ group of 4

           = _____ + _____

           = _____

10.   5 × 6 = _____

           7 × 6 = _____ groups of 6

           = 5 groups of 6 + _____ groups of 6

           = _____ + _____

           = _____

11.   10 × 6 = _____

           8 × 6 = _____ groups of 6

           = 10 groups of 6 − _____ groups of 6

           = _____ − _____

           = _____

Multiply and match.

12.

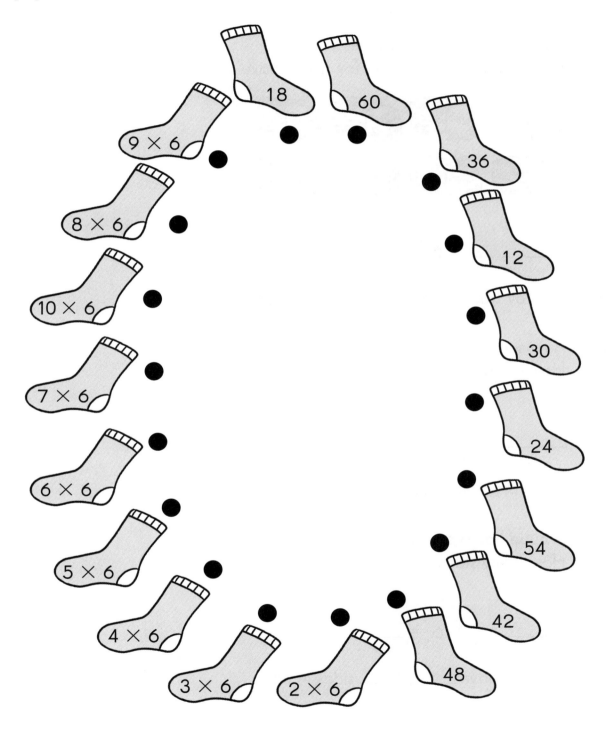

Solve.

13. James has 8 toy trucks.
Each toy truck has 6 wheels.
How many wheels do the toy trucks have in all?

_____ × 6 = _____

The toy trucks have _____ wheels in all.

14. An insect has 6 legs.
How many legs do 4 insects have?

_____ × _____ = _____

4 insects have _____ legs.

15. A cube has 6 sides.
How many sides do 9 cubes have in all?

_____ × 6 = _____

9 cubes have _____ sides in all.

Practice 3   Multiply by 7

Look at each area model. Write the multiplication fact.

Example

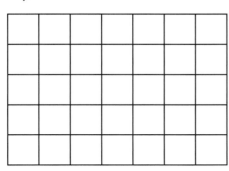

_____5_____ × _____7_____ = _____35_____

1.

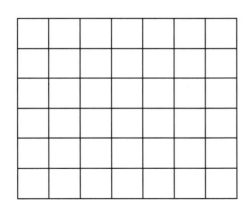

_____ × _____ = _____

2.

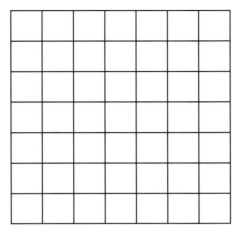

_____ × _____ = _____

Fill in the missing numbers.

3. 6 sevens = 6 × _____

4. 9 × 7 = _____ sevens

5. 5 + 5 + 5 + 5 + 5 + 5 + 5 = 7 × _____

6. 7 + 7 + 7 + 7 + 7 = 5 × _____

7. 10 × 7 = 7 × _____

8. 4 sevens = 7 + 7 + 7 + _____

Multiply. Use multiplication facts you know to find other multiplication facts.

9. 7 × 4 = 5 groups of 4 + _____ groups of 4

      = _____ + _____

      = _____

10. 5 × 7 = _____

      7 × 7 = 5 groups of 7 + _____ groups of 7

      = _____ + _____

      = _____

11. 10 × 7 = _____

      9 × 7 = 10 groups of 7 − _____ group of 7

      = _____ − _____

      = _____

Multiply and match.

12.

 49

 2 × 7

 56

 6 × 7

 70

 5 × 7

 35

 3 × 7

 21

 8 × 7

 14

 7 × 7

 42

 9 × 7

 28

 10 × 7

 4 × 7

 63

Solve.

13.   Mrs. Thompson buys 2 books.
Each book costs $7.
How much does Mrs. Thompson pay in all?

2 × $7 = $_____

Mrs. Thompson pays $_____ in all.

14.   A box contains 7 crayons.
Alex packs 10 such boxes into his bag.
How many crayons does Alex have in all?

10 × 7 = _____

Alex has _____ crayons in all.

15.   Mr. Dean gives each student 7 okras in art class.
How many okras does he give 4 students?

4 × 7 = _____

He gives 4 students _____ okras.

Practice 4   Multiply by 8

Complete the multiplication fact. Then show on the number line.

1. $3 \times 8 =$ _____

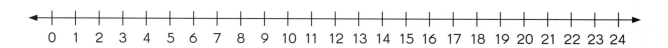

0 1 2 3 4 5 6 7 8 9 10 11 12 13 14 15 16 17 18 19 20 21 22 23 24

Complete the multiplication fact. Then shade to show on the area model.

2. $6 \times 8 =$ _____

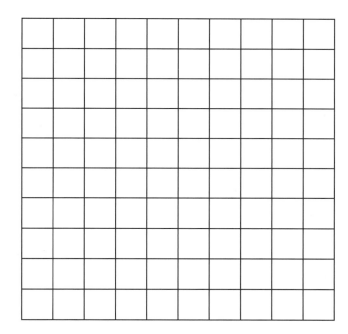

Fill in the missing numbers.

3.   8 eights $= 8 \times$ _____

4.   3 eights $=$ _____ $\times 8$

5. $6 + 6 + 6 + 6 + 6 + 6 + 6 + 6 = 8 \times$ _____

6. $8 + 8 + 8 + 8 + 8 + 8 = 6 \times$ _____

7. $5 \times 8 = 8 \times$ _____

8. 5 eights $= 8 + 8 +$ _____ $+$ _____ $+$ _____

Multiply. Use multiplication facts you know to find other multiplication facts.

9. $8 \times 4 = 10$ groups of $4 -$ _____ groups of 4

$=$ _____ $-$ _____

$=$ _____

10. $10 \times 8 =$ _____

$8 \times 8 =$ _____ groups of 8

$= 10$ groups of $8 -$ _____ groups of 8

$=$ _____ $-$ _____

$=$ _____

11. $5 \times 8 =$ _____

$7 \times 8 =$ _____ groups of 8

$= 5$ groups of $8 +$ _____ groups of 8

$=$ _____ $+$ _____

$=$ _____

Multiply and match.

12.

2 × 8	●		●	40
5 × 8	●		●	64
6 × 8	●		●	8
3 8	●		●	24
4 × 8	●		●	16
8 8	●		●	72
9 × 8	●		●	32
7 8	●		●	48
?	●		●	56

13.   What is the missing multiplication fact? _____

Solve.

─── *Example* ───────────────────────────────

An octagon has 8 equal sides.
How many sides do 5 octagons have?

$5 \times 8 = 40$

octagon

5 octagons have ____40____ sides.

──

14. 8 children make up a team.
How many children make up 7 teams?

_____ children make up 7 teams.

15. A chocolate cake has 8 cherries.
How many cherries do 6 such cakes have?

6 such cakes have _____ cherries.

Practice 5   Multiply by 9

Complete the multiplication fact. Then show on the number line.

1. $2 \times 9 =$ _____

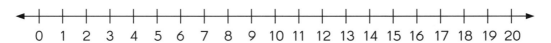

0 1 2 3 4 5 6 7 8 9 10 11 12 13 14 15 16 17 18 19 20

Complete the multiplication fact. Then show on the area model.

2. $7 \times 9 =$ _____

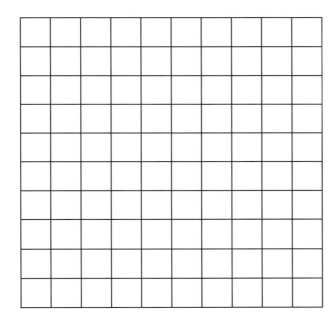

Fill in the missing numbers.

3.   3 nines $= 3 \times$ _____

4.   4 nines $=$ _____ $\times 9$

Fill in the missing numbers.

5. $9 + 9 + 9 + 9 + 9 + 9 = 6 \times$ _____

6. $6 + 6 + 6 + 6 + 6 + 6 + 6 + 6 + 6 = 9 \times$ _____

7. $9 \times 8 = 8 \times$ _____

8.   8 nines $= 9 + 9 + 9 + 9 + 9 + 9 +$ _____ $+$ _____

Use multiplication facts to help you.

9. $10 \times 4 =$ _____

$4 \times 9 = 9 \times 4$

$9 \times 4 = 10$ groups of $4 -$ _____ group of 4

$=$ _____ $-$ _____

$=$ _____

10. $10 \times 9 =$ _____

$9 \times 9 = 10$ groups of $9 -$ _____ group of 9

$=$ _____ $-$ _____

$=$ _____

11. $5 \times 9 =$ _____

$6 \times 9 = 5$ groups of $9 +$ _____ group of 9

$=$ _____ $+$ _____

$=$ _____

Match each ball to the correct basket.

12.

3×9

9×9

5×9

7 nines

36

2×9

54

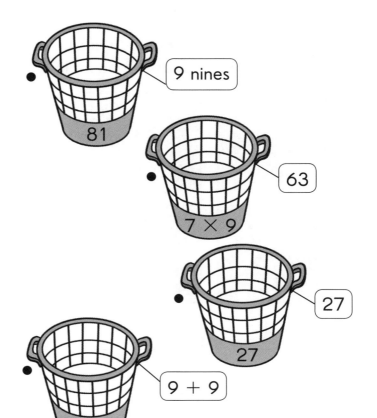

9 nines

81

63

7×9

27

27

$9 + 9$

18

$9 + 9 + 9 + 9 + 9$

45

4 nines

4×9

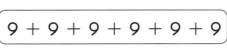

$9 + 9 + 9 + 9 + 9 + 9$

6×9

Solve.

13. Pamela pastes stickers on 4 cards.
She pastes 9 stickers on each card.
How many stickers does she paste in all?

_____ × 9 = _____

She pastes _____ stickers in all.

Use the pictures to write a multiplication story.

14.

| scissors $6 | marker $4 | pencil $2 |

_____

_____

_____

_____

Practice 6   Division: Finding the Number of Items in Each Group

Write two related division sentences.

> **Example**
>
> $6 \times 7 = 42$
>
> $42 \div$ ___6___ = ___7___
>
> $42 \div$ ___7___ = ___6___

1. $9 \times 5 = 45$

$45 \div$ _____ = _____

$45 \div$ _____ = _____

2. $7 \times 9 = 63$

$63 \div$ _____ = _____

$63 \div$ _____ = _____

3. $8 \times 6 = 48$

$48 \div$ _____ = _____

$48 \div$ _____ = _____

Fill in the missing numbers.

> *Example*
>
> $6 \times \underline{\quad 7 \quad} = 42$ So, $42 \div 6 = \underline{\quad 7 \quad}$.

4. $7 \times \underline{\hspace{2cm}} = 49$ So, $49 \div 7 = \underline{\hspace{2cm}}$.

5. $8 \times \underline{\hspace{2cm}} = 48$ So, $48 \div 8 = \underline{\hspace{2cm}}$.

6. $9 \times \underline{\hspace{2cm}} = 45$ So, $45 \div 9 = \underline{\hspace{2cm}}$.

Solve.

7.   Mrs. Brown has 9 purses with 54 coins.
Each purse has the same number of coins.
How many coins does each purse have?

$\underline{\hspace{2.5cm}} \div \underline{\hspace{2.5cm}} = \underline{\hspace{2.5cm}}$

Each purse has $\underline{\hspace{2.5cm}}$ coins.

8.   Austin collects 63 seashells.
He puts them equally into 7 boxes.
How many seashells does each box contain?

$\underline{\hspace{2.5cm}} \div \underline{\hspace{2.5cm}} = \underline{\hspace{2.5cm}}$

Each box contains $\underline{\hspace{2.5cm}}$ seashells.

Practice 7   Division: Making Equal Groups

Fill in the missing numbers.

1.   _____ × 6 = 54

     54 ÷ 6 = _____

2.   _____ × 8 = 56

     56 ÷ 8 = _____

Divide.

3.   21 ÷ 7 = _____

4.   64 ÷ 8 = _____

5.   63 ÷ 9 = _____

6.   48 ÷ 6 = _____

Solve.

7.   One tank holds 8 gallons of water.
    How many tanks are needed to hold 72 gallons of water?

    _____ ÷ _____ = _____

    _____ tanks are needed to hold 8 gallons of water each.

8.   Donald packs 36 apples into some bags.
    Each bag contains 9 apples.
    How many bags does Donald use?

    _____ ÷ _____ = _____

    Donald uses _____ bags.

 Math Journal

Solve.

1. Show 3 × 6 on the number line.

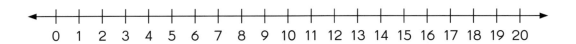

0 1 2 3 4 5 6 7 8 9 10 11 12 13 14 15 16 17 18 19 20

2. Draw an array model to show 5 × 7.

3. Show 8 × 9 with the area model.

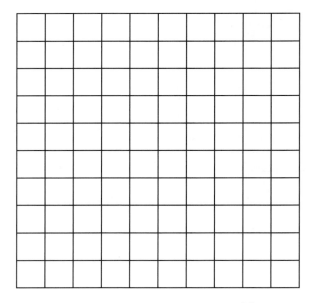

Put On Your Thinking Cap!

Challenging Practice

Complete each skip-counting pattern.

1.   70 63 56 _____ _____ 35

   _____ _____ 14 7

2.   80 72 64 _____ _____ _____

   _____ _____ 16 8

Identify a number that does not belong in the group.
Then write the reason.
Use the number patterns to help you.

3.

Number: _____

Reason: _____

_____

_____

4.

Number: _____

Reason: _____

_____

_____

 # Put On Your Thinking Cap!

Problem Solving

1. I am a two-digit number.
    I am less than 50.
    Count in sixes and you will find me!
    Divide my tens digit by 2 and you will find my ones digit.
    What am I?

Make a systematic list as shown below to help you.

Number	Tens digit	Ones digit	Check
12	1	2	✗
12 + 6 =			

I am _____.

Chapter 7 **Multiplication**

Practice 1   Mental Multiplication

Multiply mentally. Fill in the missing numbers.

Example

> Find 4×7.
>
> 4×7 is the same as 7×4.
>
> So, $4 \times 7 =$ _____28_____.

I skip-count in fours.

1.   Find 3×9.

   3×9 is the same as 9×3.

   So, $3 \times 9 =$ _____.

2.   Find 5×7.

   5×7 is the same as 7×5.

   So, $5 \times 7 =$ _____.

3.   Find 9×8.

   9×8 is the same as 8×9.

   So, $9 \times 8 =$ _____.

Multiply mentally. Fill in the missing numbers.

Example

$3 \times 50 = 3 \times 5$ tens

$= \underline{\quad 15 \quad}$ tens

$= \underline{\quad 150 \quad}$

4. $3 \times 500 = 3 \times 5$ hundreds

$= \underline{\qquad}$ hundreds

$= \underline{\qquad}$

5. $7 \times 40 = 7 \times 4$ tens

$= \underline{\qquad}$ tens

$= \underline{\qquad}$

6. $7 \times 400 = 7 \times 4$ hundreds

$= \underline{\qquad}$ hundreds

$= \underline{\qquad}$

7. $8 \times 60 = 8 \times 6$ tens

$= \underline{\qquad}$ tens

$= \underline{\qquad}$

8. $8 \times 600 = 8 \times 6$ hundreds

$= \underline{\qquad}$ hundreds

$= \underline{\qquad}$

Multiply mentally.

9. $9 \times 20 = \underline{\qquad}$

10. $9 \times 200 = \underline{\qquad}$

11. $2 \times 70 = \underline{\qquad}$

12. $2 \times 700 = \underline{\qquad}$

13. $8 \times 30 = \underline{\qquad}$

14. $8 \times 300 = \underline{\qquad}$

Practice 2   Multiplying Without Regrouping

Fill in the missing numbers.

Example

$2 \times 13 = ?$

$2 \times \underline{\quad 3 \quad}$ ones $= \underline{\quad 6 \quad}$ ones

$$\begin{array}{r} 1\ 3 \\ \times\ \ \ 2 \\ \hline \boxed{2\ 6} \end{array}$$

$2 \times \underline{\quad 1 \quad}$ ten $\ = \underline{\quad 2 \quad}$ tens

So, $2 \times 13 = \underline{\quad 26 \quad}$.

1. $2 \times 342 = ?$

$2 \times \underline{\qquad}$ ones $\quad = \underline{\qquad}$ ones

$2 \times \underline{\qquad}$ tens $\quad = \underline{\qquad}$ tens

$$\begin{array}{r} 3\ 4\ 2 \\ \times\ \ \ \ \ \ 2 \\ \hline \boxed{} \end{array}$$

$2 \times \underline{\qquad}$ hundreds $= \underline{\qquad}$ hundreds

So, $2 \times 342 = \underline{\qquad}$.

2. $3 \times 312 = ?$

$3 \times$ _____ ones $=$ _____ ones

$3 \times$ _____ ten $=$ _____ tens

$3 \times$ _____ hundreds $=$ _____ hundreds

So, $3 \times 312 =$ _____.

$$\begin{array}{r} 3\ 1\ 2 \\ \times\qquad 3 \\ \hline \boxed{} \end{array}$$

3. $4 \times 201 = ?$

$4 \times$ _____ one $=$ _____ ones

$4 \times$ _____ tens $=$ _____ tens

$4 \times$ _____ hundreds $=$ _____ hundreds

So, $4 \times 201 =$ _____.

$$\begin{array}{r} 2\ 0\ 1 \\ \times\qquad 4 \\ \hline \boxed{} \end{array}$$

© 2018 Marshall Cavendish Education Pte Ltd

Name: _____ **Date:** _____

Multiply.

```
┌─ Example ──────────────────┐
│          4  1  4           │
│      ×         2           │
│      ┌──────────────┐      │
│      │   8  2  8    │      │
│      └──────────────┘      │
└────────────────────────────┘
```

4.
```
      3  2  1
  ×         3
  ┌──────────────┐
  │              │
  └──────────────┘
```

5.
```
      1  0  2
  ×         4
  ┌──────────────┐
  │              │
  └──────────────┘
```

6.
```
      1  0  1
  ×         5
  ┌──────────────┐
  │              │
  └──────────────┘
```

Match each caterpillar to its leaf.

7.

646  • • 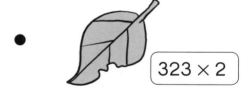 201 × 3

408  • •  323 × 2

603  • •  222 × 4

888 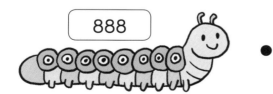 • • 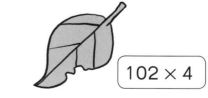 102 × 4

Multiply and complete.

8. Frederick Frog is hungry.
He is out hunting for his lunch.
Clever Frederick Frog eats only non-poisonous flies.
Flies carrying a product greater than 400 are non-poisonous.
Which flies should Frederick Frog eat?

Frederick Frog should eat flies _____.

Solve.

> ### Example
>
> Curtis scores 22 points in a game.
> He wants to score the same number of points for every game.
> How many points does he hope to score in 4 games?
>
> $22 \times 4 = 88$
>
> $$\begin{array}{r} 2\ 2 \\ \times \quad 4 \\ \hline 8\ 8 \end{array}$$
>
> He hopes to score 88 points in 4 games.

9.   143 people ride the train every hour.
How many people ride the train in 2 hours?

10.   A bakery sells 213 muffins a day.
How many muffins does it sell in 3 days?

11. A website has 232 hits in the first week.
In the second week, the website has the same number of hits.
How many hits does the website have in both weeks?

12. A grocery store sells 202 cartons of milk a week.
How many cartons of milk does it sell in 4 weeks?

Practice 3   Multiplying Ones, Tens, and Hundreds with Regrouping

Fill in the missing numbers.

> **Example**
>
> $3 \times 26 = ?$
>
> | Step 1 | Multiply the ones by 3. |
>
> $3 \times \underline{6}$ ones $= \underline{18}$ ones
>
> $$\begin{array}{r} \boxed{1} \\ 2\ \ 6 \\ \times \quad 3 \\ \hline \boxed{7\ \ 8} \end{array}$$
>
> Regroup the ones.
>
> $\underline{18}$ ones $= \underline{1}$ ten $\underline{8}$ ones
>
> | Step 2 | Multiply the tens by 3. |
>
> $3 \times \underline{2}$ tens $= \underline{6}$ tens
>
> Add the tens.
>
> $\underline{1}$ ten $+ \underline{6}$ tens $= \underline{7}$ tens
>
> So, $3 \times 26 = \underline{78}$.

Fill in the missing numbers.

1. $5 \times 16 = ?$

| Step 1 | Multiply the ones by 5.

$5 \times$ _____ ones $=$ _____ ones

Regroup the ones.

_____ ones $=$ _____ tens _____ ones

| Step 2 | Multiply the tens by 5.

$5 \times$ _____ ten $=$ _____ tens

Add the tens.

_____ tens $+$ _____ tens $=$ _____ tens

So, $5 \times 16 =$ _____.

Fill in the missing numbers.

2.   4 × 82 = ?

$$
\begin{array}{r}
8\ 2 \\
\times\ \ \ 4 \\
\hline
\end{array}
$$

| Step 1 | Multiply the ones by 4. |

4 × _____ ones = _____ ones

| Step 2 | Multiply the tens by 4. |

4 × _____ tens = _____ tens

Regroup the tens.

_____ tens = _____ hundreds _____ tens

So, 4 × 82 = _____.

Fill in the missing numbers.

3. $5 \times 78 = ?$

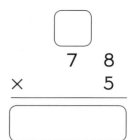

$$\begin{array}{r} 7\ 8 \\ \times\ \ \ \ 5 \\ \hline \end{array}$$

Step 1   Multiply the ones by 5.

$5 \times$ _____ ones = _____ ones

Regroup the ones.

_____ ones = _____ tens _____ ones

Step 2   Multiply the tens by 5.

$5 \times$ _____ tens = _____ tens

Add the tens.

_____ tens + _____ tens = _____ tens

Regroup the tens.

_____ tens = _____ hundreds _____ tens

So, $5 \times 78 =$ _____.

Fill in the missing numbers.

4. $4 \times 115 = ?$

$$
\begin{array}{r}
\boxed{} \\
1 \quad 1 \quad 5 \\
\times \qquad 4 \\
\hline
\boxed{}
\end{array}
$$

Step 1   Multiply the ones by 4.

$4 \times$ _____ ones $=$ _____ ones

Regroup the ones.

_____ ones $=$ _____ tens _____ ones

Step 2   Multiply the tens by 4.

$4 \times$ _____ ten $=$ _____ tens

Add the tens.

_____ tens $+$ _____ tens $=$ _____ tens

Step 3   Multiply the hundreds.

$4 \times$ _____ hundred $=$ _____ hundreds

So, $4 \times 115 =$ _____ .

Fill in the missing numbers.

5. $4 \times 242 = ?$

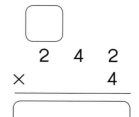

Step 1 Multiply the ones by 4.

$4 \times$ _____ ones = _____ ones

Step 2 Multiply the tens by 4.

$4 \times$ _____ tens = _____ tens

Regroup the tens.

_____ tens = _____ hundred _____ tens

Step 3 Multiply the hundreds by 4.

$4 \times$ _____ hundreds = _____ hundreds

Add the hundreds.

_____ hundred + _____ hundreds

= _____ hundreds

So, $4 \times 242 =$ _____ .

Fill in the missing numbers.

6.   5 × 145 = ?

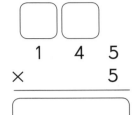

$$\begin{array}{r} 1\ \ 4\ \ 5 \\ \times 5 \\ \hline \end{array}$$

Step 1   Multiply the ones by 5.

5 × _____ ones = _____ ones

Regroup the ones.

_____ ones = _____ tens _____ ones

Step 2   Multiply the tens by 5.

5 × _____ tens = _____ tens

Add the tens.

_____ tens + _____ tens = _____ tens

Regroup the tens.

_____ tens = _____ hundreds _____ tens

Step 3   Multiply the hundreds by 5.

5 × _____ hundred = _____ hundreds

Add the hundreds.

_____ hundreds + _____ hundreds

= _____ hundreds

So, 5 × 145 = _____.

Fill in the missing numbers.

7. $5 \times 159 = ?$

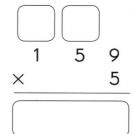

Step 1	Multiply the ones by 5.

$5 \times$ _____ ones = _____ ones

Regroup the ones.

_____ ones = _____ tens _____ ones

Step 2	Multiply the tens by 5.

$5 \times$ _____ tens = _____ tens

Add the tens.

_____ tens + _____ tens = _____ tens

Regroup the tens.

_____ tens = _____ hundreds _____ tens

Step 3	Multiply the hundreds by 5.

$5 \times$ _____ hundred = _____ hundreds

Add the hundreds.

_____ hundreds + _____ hundreds

= _____ hundreds

So, $5 \times 159 =$ _____.

Practice 4 Multiplying Ones, Tens, and Hundreds with Regrouping

Multiply and complete.

1.

Example

3 5
× 5
———
1 7 5 **K**

4 8 6
× 2
———
D

2 7 9
× 3
———
Y

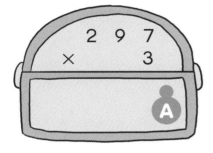

2 9 7
× 3
———
A

3 0 4
× 3
———
L

1 5 6
× 4
———
O

2 4 8
× 4
———
N

1 5 5
× 5
———
Z

1 9 9
× 5
———
E

What key cannot unlock treasure chests?

Write the letters which match the answers to find out.

____	____	____	K	____	____
972	624	992	175	995	837

Solve.

> **Example**
>
> Gina reads 84 pages of her book in a day.
> How many pages does Gina read in 5 days?
>
> $84 \times 5 = 420$
>
> Gina reads 420 pages in 5 days.

2. 187 cars are in a parking lot.
Each car has 4 wheels.
How many wheels do the cars have in all?

3. 198 students attend a school.
Each student carries 3 books.
How many books do they carry in all?

4. Jill feeds her pet hamster 5 food pellets each day.
How many food pellets does she feed her hamster in 165 days?

Multiply.

5. $450 \times 2 =$ _____

6. $232 \times 4 =$ _____

7. $259 \times 3 =$ _____

8. $196 \times 5 =$ _____

Complete.

9.   Circle the chest with the greatest product.

10.   Underline the chest with the least product.

   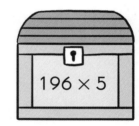

450 × 2   232 × 4   259 × 3   196 × 5

Solve.
Then circle the chest with the correct answer.

11.   Keith runs from Tree A to B to C, to D to E, then to F.
The trees are planted 134 meters apart from each other.
How far does Keith run in all?

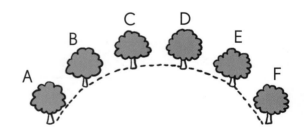

Keith runs _____ meters in all.

560   670   760   650

Math Journal

Write the steps to your answer.

Multiply 243 by 2.

Example

Step 1	Multiply 3 ones by 2. 2×3 ones $= 6$ ones	$$\begin{array}{r} 2\ 4\ 3 \\ \times\ 2 \\ \hline \boxed{6} \end{array}$$
Step 2	Multiply 4 tens by 2. 2×4 tens $= 8$ tens	$$\begin{array}{r} 2\ 4\ 3 \\ \times\ 2 \\ \hline \boxed{8\ 6} \end{array}$$
Step 3	Multiply 2 hundreds by 2. 2×2 hundreds $= 4$ hundreds	$$\begin{array}{r} 2\ 4\ 3 \\ \times\ 2 \\ \hline \boxed{4\ 8\ 6} \end{array}$$

So, $2 \times 243 = 486$.

Multiply 323 by 3.

$$\begin{array}{r} 3\ 2\ 3 \\ \times\ 3 \\ \hline \boxed{} \end{array}$$

Step 1 _____

_____

Step 2 _____

_____

Step 3 _____

_____

Put On Your Thinking Cap!

Challenging Practice

Fill in the missing numbers.

1.
```
    2 ☐
  ×   2
  ─────
    4 8
```

2.
```
    1 7
  ×   ☐
  ─────
    6 8
```

3.
```
  ☐ 3 1
  ×     3
  ───────
    6 9 3
```

4.
```
    1 2 1
  ×     ☐
  ───────
    6 0 5
```

5.
```
    3 0 8
  ×     ☐
  ───────
    6 1 6
```

6.
```
    1 ☐ 5
  ×     4
  ───────
    5 4 0
```

7.
```
    ☐ 5 2
  ×     3
  ───────
    7 5 6
```

8.
```
    1 ☐ 8
  ×     4
  ───────
    5 9 2
```

Put On Your Thinking Cap!

Problem Solving

Solve.

Frank has 100 geese and cows on his farm.
The animals have a total of 340 legs.
How many geese and cows does Frank have?

Guess and check your answer.

Geese (2 legs)	Cows (4 legs)	Total number of legs	Correct (✓) / Wrong (✗)
50 × 2 = 100	50 × 4 = 200	100 + 200 = 300	✗
60 × 2 = 120	40 × 4 = 160	120 + 160 = 280	✗

Frank has _____ geese and _____ cows.

Cumulative Review

for Chapters 6 and 7

Concepts and Skills

Fill in the blanks. *(Lessons 6.1 to 6.5)*

1. _____ $\times 8 = 0$

2. _____ $\times 1 = 7$

3. 9 sixes $= 9 \times$ _____

4. $4 \times 7 =$ _____ sevens

5. $3 \times 6 = 6 + 6 +$ _____

6. $7 \times 6 = 6 \times$ _____

7. $9 \times$ _____ $= 0$

8. $8 + 8 + 8 + 8 + 8 = 5 \times$ _____

9. 5 nines $+ 3$ nines $=$ _____ $\times 9$

10. $9 + 9 + 9 + 9 =$ _____ nines

Complete each multiplication fact.
Then show on the number line. *(Lessons 6.1 and 6.4)*

11. $2 \times 4 \times 3 = ?$

Step 1   _____ $\times$ 4 = _____

Step 2   _____ $\times$ 3 = _____

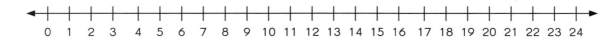

So, $2 \times 4 \times 3 =$ _____ $\times$ _____

= _____.

12. $2 \times 4 \times 3 = ?$

Step 1   _____ $\times$ 3 = _____

Step 2 $2 \times$ _____ = _____

So, $2 \times 4 \times 3 =$ _____ $\times$ _____

= _____.

Name: _____   **Date:** _____

Multiply. Use multiplication facts you know to find other multiplication facts. *(Lessons 6.3 and 6.5)*

13. $5 \times 7 =$ _____

So, $6 \times 7 =$ _____ groups of 7 $+$ _____ group of 7

$=$ _____ $+$ _____

$=$ _____

14. $10 \times 9 =$ _____

So, $8 \times 9 =$ _____ groups of 9 $-$ _____ groups of 9

$=$ _____ $-$ _____

$=$ _____

Write two related division sentences. *(Lessons 6.3, 6.4, 6.5 and 6.6)*

15. $8 \times 4 =$ _____

_____ $\div$ _____ $=$ _____

_____ $\div$ _____ $=$ _____

16.   _____ $\times$ _____ $=$ _____

$54 \div$ _____ $= 9$

_____ $\div$ _____ $=$ _____

Multiply. Fill in the missing numbers. *(Lesson 7.1)*

17. $4 \times 9 =$ _____

$4 \times 90 = 4 \times$ _____ tens

$=$ _____ tens

$=$ _____

18. $10 \times 7 =$ _____

$10 \times 700 = 10 \times$ _____ hundreds

$=$ _____ hundreds

$=$ _____

Multiply. Use mental math. *(Lesson 7.1)*

19. $10 \times 3 =$ _____

20. $5 \times 10 =$ _____

21. $20 \times 4 =$ _____

22. $3 \times 40 =$ _____

23. $500 \times 2 =$ _____

24. $4 \times 200 =$ _____

Multiply. Show your work. *(Lessons 7.2 and 7.3)*

25. $212 \times 4 =$ _____

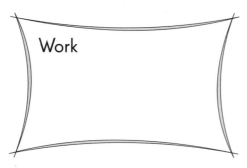

Work

26. $148 \times 5 =$ _____

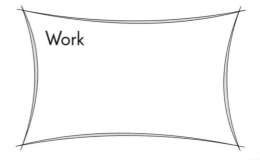

Work

27.

```
    4 3 2
  ×     2
```

28.

```
    2 5 1
  ×     3
```

Problem Solving

Solve. Show your work.

29. Cheryl completes 42 pages of math exercises.
There are 4 exercises on each page.
How many exercises does she complete?

30. Damien has 48 marbles.
He packs all the marbles equally into 8 bags.
How many marbles are there in each bag?

31. Mr. Roberts has 63 daisies and some pots.
He plants 9 daisies in each pot.
How many pots does he use?

32. A farmer packs 49 pounds of grain into 7-pound bags.
How many bags does the farmer need?

33. A grocer sells 153 bags of carrots.
Each bag has 5 carrots.
How many carrots does the grocer sell?

34. Jessie buys 4 cartons of markers.
Each carton contains 125 markers.
How many markers does she buy?

Division

Practice 1   Mental Division

**Think of the multiplication facts for 6, 7, 8, and 9.
Then fill in the blanks.**

> *Example*
>
> _____6_____ × 6 = 36   36 ÷ 6 = _____6_____

1. _____ × 7 = 35   35 ÷ 7 = _____

2. _____ × 8 = 72   72 ÷ 8 = _____

3. _____ × 9 = 63   63 ÷ 9 = _____

4. _____ × 9 = 81   81 ÷ 9 = _____

Fill in the blanks.

5. $56 \div 7 =$ _____ ones $\div$ 7

   $=$ _____ ones

   $=$ _____

6. $360 \div 9 =$ _____ tens $\div$ 9

   $=$ _____ tens

   $=$ _____

7. $600 \div 3 =$ _____ hundreds $\div$ 3

   $=$ _____ hundreds

   $=$ _____

8. $4,500 \div 5 =$ _____ hundreds $\div$ 5

   $=$ _____ hundreds

   $=$ _____

Divide. Use related multiplication facts and patterns to help you.

9. $240 \div 4 =$ _____   **10.** $250 \div 5 =$ _____

11. $180 \div 9 =$ _____   **12.** $180 \div 6 =$ _____

13. $320 \div 8 =$ _____   **14.** $490 \div 7 =$ _____

Practice 2   Quotient and Remainder

Fill in the blanks. Use repeated subtraction to help you.

1.   24 ones ÷ 3 = _____ R _____

Quotient   = _____ ones

Remainder   = _____ ones

2.   22 ones ÷ 4 = _____ R _____

Quotient   = _____ ones

Remainder   = _____ ones

Find the quotient. Use related multiplication facts to help you.

┌─ *Example* ─────────────────┐

27 ÷ 3 = [9]

└──────────────────────────────┘

3.   20 ÷ 4 = [ ]

4.   24 ÷ 4 = [ ]

5.   40 ÷ 5 = [ ]

6.   32 ÷ 4 = [ ]

7.   24 ÷ 3 = [ ]

8.   50 ÷ 5 = [ ]

9.   18 ÷ 2 = [ ]

Divide. Use repeated subtraction or related multiplication facts to help you.
The remainder is the number of eyes each character has.
Draw the correct number of eyes for each character.

Example

$6 \times 3 = 18$
$7 \times 3 = 21$
$8 \times 3 = 24$
Choose [7] as the quotient.

$23 \div 3$

Quotient = ___7___ ones

Remainder = ___2___ ones

10.

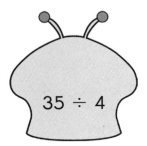

$35 \div 4$

Quotient = _____ ones

Remainder = _____ ones

11.

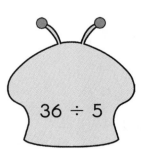

$36 \div 5$

Quotient = _____ ones

Remainder = _____ one

12.

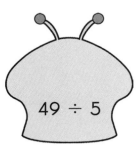

$49 \div 5$

Quotient = _____ ones

Remainder = _____ ones

Name: _____ **Date:** _____

Practice 3   Odd and Even Numbers

Look at the picture. Then answer the question.
Explain your answer.

1. Is 21 an even number? _____

Explain your answer.

_____

2. Is 32 an odd number? _____

Explain your answer.

_____

Divide.

3. 14 ÷ 2 = [   ] R [   ]

4. 23 ÷ 2 = [   ] R [   ]

5. 29 ÷ 2 = [   ] R [   ]

Use your answers in Questions 3, 4, and 5 to answer Questions 6 and 7.

6. _____ is an even number.

It does not have a _____ when divided by 2.

7. _____ and _____ are odd numbers.

They have a _____ of _____ when divided by 2.

Look at the numbers in the box. Then answer the questions.

11	30	68	76	59	95
84	92	123	477	980	

8. Circle the **even numbers** and write them on the line below.

_____

9. Write the **odd numbers**. _____

10. Write the ones digit in the even numbers in Question 8. _____

11. Write the ones digit in the odd numbers in Question 9. _____

Fill in the blanks.

12. Use the digits to make the greatest 4-digit **odd number**.   4 5 2 9   _____

13. Use the digits to make the least 4-digit **even number**.   0 1 6 9   _____
(Do not begin with zero.)

Practice 4   Division Without Remainder and Regrouping

Divide. Then match the answers to the correct pictures.

Tens	Ones
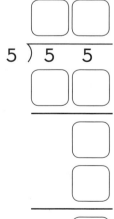	

1.   44 ones ÷ 4 = _____ ten _____ one •   •

2.   69 ones ÷ 3 = _____ tens _____ ones •   •

Divide.

3.

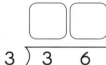

3) 3   6

4.

4) 8   4

5.

5) 5   5

Divide.
Then draw a line from each tree to the bird with the matching quotient.

6.

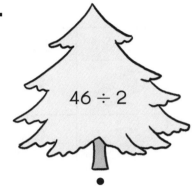 $46 \div 2$

 $96 \div 3$

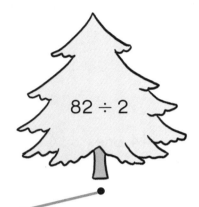 $82 \div 2$

 41

 23

 13

 32

 11

 21

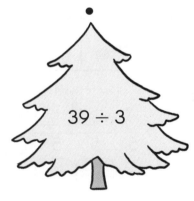 $39 \div 3$

 $44 \div 4$

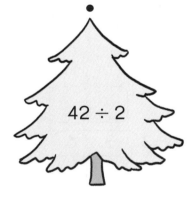 $42 \div 2$

Practice 5   Division with Regrouping in Tens and Ones

Divide. Use base-ten blocks to help you.

1.
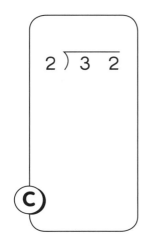
$2\overline{)3\ 2}$
C

2.
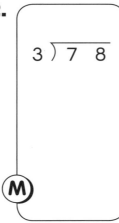
$3\overline{)7\ 8}$
M

3.
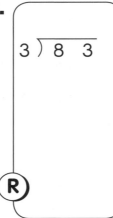
$3\overline{)8\ 3}$
R

4.
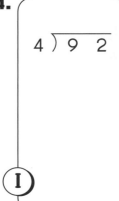
$4\overline{)9\ 2}$
I

5.
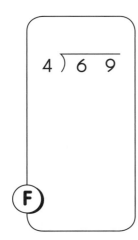
$4\overline{)6\ 9}$
F

6.
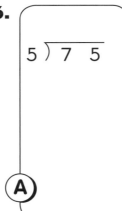
$5\overline{)7\ 5}$
A

7.
$5\overline{)6\ 3}$
T

8.
$2\overline{)7\ 2}$
J

What kind of jam cannot be eaten?

Match the letters to the quotients below to find out.

9.

____ ____ ____   ____ ____ ____ ____   ____ ____ ____
12   27   15   17   17   23   16   36   15   26

Math Journal

Write *True* or *False*.
If the statement is false, rewrite the sentence to make it true.

1. When I divide one number by another, the answer is called a remainder. Any number left is called a quotient.

    _____

    _____

    _____

2. When an odd number is divided by 2, there is no remainder.

    _____

    _____

3. When an even number is divided by 2, there is a remainder.

    _____

    _____

4. I always divide the ones first, then the tens for the following:

    $3 \overline{)3\ 2}$ $4 \overline{)2\ 6}$ $5 \overline{)7\ 1}$

    _____

    _____

Put On Your Thinking Cap!

Challenging Practice

Solve.

1. Find the sum of all the odd numbers between 60 and 66.

2. Which of these division statements are true?
Color them.

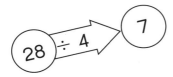

28 ÷ 4 → 7

19 ÷ 5 → 4

18 ÷ 4 → 4

75 ÷ 5 → 15

63 ÷ 3 → 21

85 ÷ 5 → 17

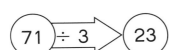

71 ÷ 3 → 23

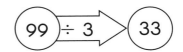

99 ÷ 3 → 33

Put On Your Thinking Cap!

Problem Solving

Solve.

Mrs. Jones has some coloring books to give away as gifts.

She has fewer than 60 but more than 40 coloring books.

She will have 2 coloring books left over if she divides them equally among 10 children.

She will also have 2 coloring books left over if she divides them equally among 8 children.

How many coloring books does she have?

Use the table to help you.

Check (✓) or cross (✗) the last column to show whether the answer is correct.

The first two rows are done for you.

Number of Coloring Books	Divide Among 10 Children	Divide Among 8 Children	Correct ?
59	5 R 9	7 R 3	✗
52	5 R 2	6 R 4	✗
48			

Mrs. Jones has _____ coloring books.

© 2018 Marshall Cavendish Education Pte Ltd

Name: _____   Date: _____

Chapter 9 Using Bar Models: Multiplication and Division

Practice 1 Real-World Problems: Multiplication

Solve. Use bar models to help you.

> *Example*
>
> Carlos bakes 42 muffins.
> Kim bakes twice as many muffins as Carlos.
> How many muffins does Kim bake?
>
>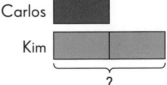
>
> $42 \times 2 =$ ___*84*___
>
> Kim bakes ___*84*___ muffins.

1. Mrs. Bently pays $95 for a new bed.
Mrs. Lee pays three times as much as Mrs. Bently for a new bed.
How much does Mrs. Lee pay for the new bed?

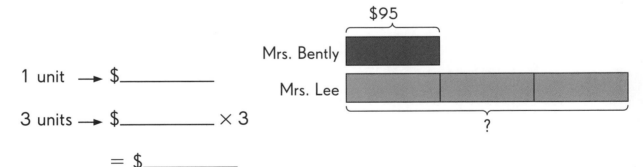

1 unit ⟶ $_____

3 units ⟶ $_____ × 3

  = $_____

Mrs. Lee pays $_____ for a new bed.

Solve. Draw bar models to help you.

2. Mr. Suarez drove 98 miles on his vacation this year.
He drove 4 times that distance last year.
How far did Mr. Suarez drive on his vacation last year?

_____ ◯ _____ = _____

Mr. Suarez drove _____ miles on his vacation last year.

3. School A collects 76 bundles of newspaper for recycling.
School B collects 5 times the number of bundles as School A.
How many bundles of newspaper does School B collect?

Name: _____ **Date:** _____

Practice 2   Real-World Problems:
Two-Step Problems with Multiplication

Solve. Use bar models to help you.

Example
---

6 boys and 4 girls are in the chorus.
Each chorus member has 8 concert tickets to sell.

a. How many members are in the chorus?

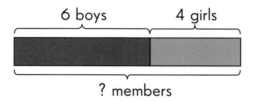

6 boys   4 girls

? members

_____6_____ $\left(+\right)$ _____4_____ = _____10_____

There are _____10_____ members in the chorus.

b. How many concert tickets do they have in all?

8 tickets

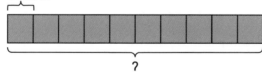

?

_____10_____ $\left(\times\right)$ _____8_____ = _____80_____

They have _____80_____ concert tickets in all.

Solve. Use the letters *a* and *b* to represent the unknown numbers. Use bar models to help you.

Example

There are 5 cookies in each box.
Jonathan packed 7 boxes of cookies.
He then had 29 cookies left.

a. How many cookies did Jonathan pack in the boxes in all?

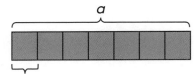

a

5 cookies

$$\underline{\quad 7 \quad} \times \underline{\quad 5 \quad} = \underline{\quad a \quad}$$

$$\underline{\quad a \quad} = \underline{\quad 35 \quad}$$

Jonathan packed _____35_____ cookies into the boxes.

b. How many cookies did Jonathan have at first?

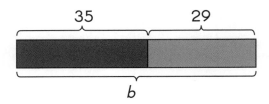

35   29

b

$$\underline{\quad 35 \quad} + \underline{\quad 29 \quad} = \underline{\quad b \quad}$$

$$\underline{\quad b \quad} = \underline{\quad 64 \quad}$$

Jonathan had _____64_____ cookies at first.

Solve. Use the letters *c* and *d* to represent the unknown numbers. Draw bar models to help you.

1. Aileen has 8 packets of gingerbread men.
There are 2 gingerbread men in each packet.
Christine then gives Aileen another 61 gingerbread men.

    a. How many gingerbread men does Aileen have at first?

_____ $\bigcirc$ _____ = _____

_____ = _____

Aileen has _____ gingerbread men at first.

    b. How many gingerbread men does Aileen have now?

_____ $\bigcirc$ _____ = _____

_____ = _____

Aileen has _____ gingerbread men now.

Solve. Use the letters *h* and *j* to represent the unknown numbers. Draw bar models to help you.

2. There are 10 rows of chairs in a hall.
    Each row has 9 chairs.
    Peter painted 34 chairs in the hall yesterday.
    How many chairs in the hall are yet to be painted?

_____ ◯ _____ = _____

_____ = _____

_____ ◯ _____ = _____

_____ = _____

_____ chairs in the hall are yet to be painted.

Solve. Draw bar models to help you.

3. The school cafeteria sells 88 cartons of milk in a month.
    It sells 4 times as many bottles of water.

    a. How many bottles of water does the cafeteria sell?

_____ ◯ _____ = _____

The cafeteria sells _____ bottles of water.

    b. How many more bottles of water than cartons of milk
    does the cafeteria sell?

_____ ◯ _____ = _____

The cafeteria sells _____ more bottles of water than
cartons of milk.

Solve. Draw bar models to help you.

4. A museum has 75 carvings in its collection.
It has 10 more pieces of pottery than carvings.
It has 3 times as many paintings as pieces of pottery.
How many paintings does the museum have?

First, I _____.

Then, I _____.

Solve. Draw bar models to help you.

5.   The second graders collect 65 books for a charity book drive.
They put some of the books in boxes and have 25 books left to pack.
The third graders have 4 times as many books in boxes.
There are none left to pack.
How many books do the third graders collect?

First, I _____.

Then, I _____.

Solve. Draw bar models to help you.

6.   Mary has 215 pencils.
       She wants to put 30 pencils in 8 boxes.
       How many more pencils does she need?

Solve. Draw bar models to help you.

7. A bookcase has 5 shelves.
Each shelf has 120 books.
174 books are fiction.
How many books are nonfiction?

Solve. Use bar models to help you.

8.   Eunice reads 5 times as many pages of a story book as Peter.
Kevin reads 30 more pages than Eunice.
Peter reads 25 pages.
How many pages does Kevin read?

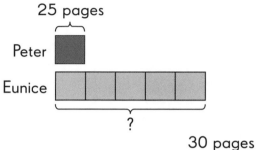

1 unit ⟶ _____

5 units ⟶ _____ ◯ _____

= _____

Eunice reads _____ pages of the story book.

_____ ◯ _____ = _____

Kevin reads _____ pages of the story book.

Solve. Draw bar models to help you.

9.   Jill has 28 stickers.
Peggy has 4 times as many stickers as Jill.
Luis has 15 fewer stickers than Peggy.
How many stickers does Luis have?

Name: _____ Date: _____

Practice 3 Real-World Problems: Division

Solve. Use bar models to help you.

--- Example ---

May has 48 flowers.
She needs 4 flowers to make each centerpiece.
How many such centerpieces can she make?

48 flowers

? centerpieces

$\underline{\quad 48 \quad} \div \underline{\quad 4 \quad} = \underline{\quad 12 \quad}$

She can make _____ 12 _____ such centerpieces.

---

1. Mr. Morton shares 75 marbles equally among 5 children.
How many marbles does each child get?

75 marbles

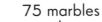

?

$\underline{\qquad} \div \underline{\qquad} = \underline{\qquad}$

Each child gets _____ marbles.

Solve. Draw bar models to help you.

2.   Cally works 63 hours in 7 weeks.
She works an equal number of hours per week.
How many hours does she work per week?

_____ ◯ _____ = _____

She works _____ hours per week.

3.   Each shirt has 8 buttons.
There are 72 buttons in all.
How many shirts are there?

_____ ◯ _____ = _____

There are _____ shirts.

Name: _____   Date: _____

Solve. Use bar models to help you.

Example

Tina gives $85 to Aiden and Nick.
Aiden gets 4 times as much money as Nick.
How much does Nick get?

Aiden

Nick

$85

5 units ———→ $_____85_____

1 unit ———→ $_____85_____ ÷ _____5_____

= $_____17_____

Nick gets $_____17_____.

4. Auntie Agnes makes 24 hotdogs.
She puts them on a round tray and a square tray.
Twice as many hotdogs are on the square tray as on the round tray.
How many more hotdogs are there on the square tray than on the round tray?

square tray

round tray

} 24 hotdogs

?

3 units ———→ _____

1 unit ———→ _____ ◯ _____

= _____

There are _____ more hotdogs on the square tray.

Solve. Draw bar models to help you.

5.   Elena takes 80 photos on her vacation.
         She takes 4 times as many photos as Luke.
         How many photos does Luke take?

6.   Mr. King picked 54 peaches from his orchard.
         He picked 9 times as many peaches as Mr. Tang.
         How many peaches did Mr. Tang pick?

Practice 4 Real-World Problems: Two-Step Problems with Division

Solve. Use bar models to help you.

Example

Katie bakes 56 pineapple tarts.
She packs 20 pineapple tarts into a plastic container.
The remaining tarts are packed equally into 6 boxes.

a. How many pineapple tarts are packed into boxes?

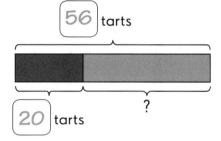

56 tarts

20 tarts

?

__56__ ⊖ __20__ = __36__

__36__ pineapple tarts are packed into boxes.

b. How many pineapple tarts are in each box?

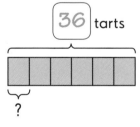

36 tarts

?

__36__ ÷ __6__ = __6__

There are __6__ pineapple tarts in each box.

Solve. Use bar models to help you.

1. A fruit seller has 64 oranges in some bags.
    Each bag has 8 oranges.
    She sells the oranges for $2 per bag.
    How much does she sell all the oranges for?

64 oranges

? bags of oranges

_____ ◯ _____ = _____

There are _____ bags of oranges.

How many bags of
oranges are there?

☐ bags of oranges

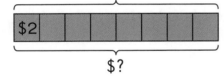

$?

_____ ◯ _____ = _____

She sells all the oranges for $_____.

First, I _____.

Then, I _____.

Name: _____   **Date:** _____

Solve. Draw bar models to help you.

2. Alex has 14 pencils.
    Lance has 4 times as many pencils as Alex.
    Lance's pencils are shared equally among 2 children.
    How many pencils does each child get?

First, I _____.

Then, I _____.

3. Richard has 90 pennies.
    He keeps 10 pennies and divides the rest
    of the pennies equally among his 4 sisters.
    How many pennies does each sister get?

First, I _____.

Then, I _____.

Solve. Draw bar models to help you.

4.   A baker makes 32 rolls in the morning.
He makes 64 rolls in the afternoon.
He packs all the rolls equally into 4 boxes.
How many rolls does each box have?

5.   Marcus collects 14 stamps each month.
Wayne collects 19 stamps each month.
How many months does Wayne take to collect 65 more stamps
than Marcus?

Solve. Use the letters *a* and *b* to represent the unknown numbers.

Example

Ms. Butler made 38 bookmarks for some students.
Mr. Fujita made 42 more bookmarks.
They distributed the bookmarks equally among 8 children.

a. How many bookmarks did they make altogether?

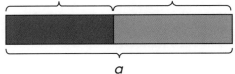

$$\underline{\quad 38 \quad} \left(+\right) \underline{\quad 42 \quad} = \underline{\quad a \quad}$$

$$\underline{\quad a \quad} = \underline{\quad 80 \quad}$$

They made ___80___ bookmarks altogether.

b. How many bookmarks did each child receive?

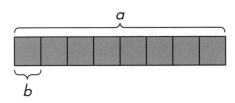

$$\underline{\quad 80 \quad} \left(\div\right) \underline{\quad 8 \quad} = \underline{\quad b \quad}$$

$$\underline{\quad b \quad} = \underline{\quad 10 \quad}$$

Each child received ___10___ bookmarks.

Solve. Use the letters *c* and *d* to represent the unknown numbers. Draw bar models to help you.

6.   Mrs. Perez baked 99 scones.
She gave 78 scones to her neighbors.
She then gave the rest to some girls.
Each girl received 3 scones.

a.   How many scones were left after Mrs. Perez gave scones to her neighbors?

_____ ◯ _____ = _____

_____ = _____

Mrs. Perez had _____ scones left.

b.   How many girls received 3 scones each?

_____ ◯ _____ = _____

_____ = _____

_____ girls received 3 scones each.

Solve. Draw bar models to help you.

7. Mary Anne bought 29 storybooks last week.
She bought another 16 storybooks this week.
She wanted to pack the storybooks into bags of 5 storybooks each.
How many bags did Mary Anne need to pack all the storybooks?

_____ ◯ _____ = _____

_____ = _____

_____ ◯ _____ = _____

_____ = _____

Mary Anne needed _____ bags for the storybooks.

Math Journal

Look at the bar models, number sentences, and the answer statement. Write a question that matches this problem.

1.

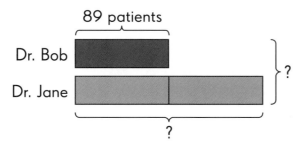

89 patients

Dr. Bob

Dr. Jane

?

?

$$3 \times 89 = 89 \times 3$$

Method 1

$89 \times 2 = 178$ or

$178 + 89 = 267$

Method 2

1 unit ⟶ 89

3 units ⟶ $3 \times 89 = 267$

Both doctors see 267 patients.

My question:

Look at the bar models and the answer statement.
Write a question that matches this problem and
show two possible methods for solving the word problem.

2.

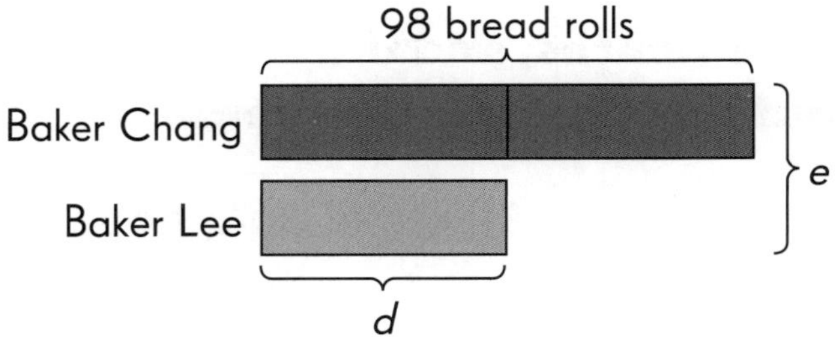

98 bread rolls

Baker Chang

Baker Lee

e

d

Both bakers bake 147 bread rolls.

My question:

My methods:

 Put On Your Thinking Cap!

 Challenging Practice

Solve. Draw bar models to help you.

1. Timmy and Pedro have 24 trading cards altogether.
Pedro has 10 fewer cards than Timmy.
After giving 5 cards to Pedro, both Timmy and Pedro have an equal number of cards.
How many trading cards does Pedro have at first?

Put On Your Thinking Cap!

Problem Solving

Solve. Use bar models to help you.

2. Johanna has some chicken nuggets and 6 sticks.
She puts 3 chicken nuggets on each stick.

She has 2 chicken nuggets left.

If she puts 4 chicken nuggets on each stick,

how many chicken nuggets will be left?

How many sticks will she need?

Cumulative Review

for Chapters 8 and 9

Concepts and Skills

Complete. Use the digits 1, 3, and 8. *(Lesson 8.3)*

1. Write two 3-digit even numbers.

even numbers
_____
_____

2. Write four 3-digit odd numbers.

odd numbers	
_____	_____
_____	_____

Fill in the blanks. Use mental math. *(Lesson 8.1)*

3. $6 \div 2 =$ _____

$60 \div 2 =$ _____ tens $\div$ 2

$=$ _____ tens

$=$ _____

$600 \div 2 =$ _____ hundreds $\div$ 2

$=$ _____ hundreds

$=$ _____

Divide. *(Lessons 8.4 and 8.5)*

4. 3$\overline{)9\ 6}$ **5.** 3$\overline{)9\ 3}$ **6.** 5$\overline{)5\ 6}$

7. 2$\overline{)7\ 3}$ **8.** 4$\overline{)4\ 7}$ **9.** 5$\overline{)9\ 8}$

Divide. Then match the division facts that have the same quotients. *(Lessons 8.1 and 8.2)*

10. 35 ÷ 5 •   • 160 ÷ 4

      27 ÷ 3 •   • 56 ÷ 8

      120 ÷ 3 •   • 36 ÷ 4

      75 ÷ 5 •   • 96 ÷ 3

      64 ÷ 2 •   • 15 ÷ 1

Problem Solving

Solve. Draw bar models to help you.

11. Roland has 125 trading cards.
Ian has three times as many trading cards as Roland.
How many trading cards does Ian have?

12. Mr. Hansen gives out 250 pencils to 5 classes.
Each class receives an equal number of pencils.
How many pencils does each class receive?

13. Mike is three times as tall as Pamela.
Pamela is 2 feet tall.
   a. How tall is Mike?

   b. How many feet taller is Mike than Pamela?

14. Mrs. Herra buys 3 boxes of oranges. She also buys 6 boxes of apples. Each box contains 65 pieces of fruit.
   a. How many boxes of fruit does Mrs. Herra buy?

   b. How many pieces of fruit does Mrs. Herra buy?

15.   Shaun has 96 ounces of lemonade.
He pours all the lemonade equally into 6 jugs.
He then pours out one of the jugs of lemonade to fill 2 glasses.
How many ounces of lemonade does each glass hold?

16.   A watch costs $56.
A camera costs double the amount of the watch.
How much do the two items cost in all?

17. Ben has 4 cartons of crayons.
Each carton contains 120 crayons.
He puts them equally into 6 cartons.
How many crayons are in each carton?

18. Natalie has 275 centimeters of ribbon to make headbands.
She makes 4 headbands and has 15 centimeters of ribbon left.
What length of ribbon does she use for each headband?

Mid-Year Review

Test Prep

Multiple Choice

Fill in the circle next to the correct answer.

1. In the number 6,592, the digit 5 is in the _____ place. *(Lesson 1.2)*

    Ⓐ ones   Ⓑ tens

    Ⓒ hundreds   Ⓓ thousands

2. Which number is 1,000 more than 1,629? *(Lesson 1.3)*

    Ⓐ 629   Ⓑ 1,619

    Ⓒ 1,729   Ⓓ 2,629

3. Estimate the sum of 342 and 525. Use front-end estimation. *(Lesson 2.5)*

    Ⓐ $300 + 500 = 800$ Ⓑ $300 + 530 = 830$

    Ⓒ $340 + 500 = 840$ Ⓓ $340 + 530 = 870$

4. Estimate the difference between 828 and 535.
Use rounding to the nearest hundred. *(Lesson 2.4)*

    Ⓐ $900 - 500 = 400$

    Ⓑ $800 - 500 = 300$

    Ⓒ $900 - 600 = 300$

    Ⓓ $800 - 600 = 200$

5. $0 \times 9 =$ _____ (Lesson 6.1)

  (A) 0   (B) 9

  (C) 90   (D) 900

6. To find the answer to 38 + 48, You can add 50 to _____. (Lesson 2.1)

  (A) 38, then add 2   (B) 38, then subtract 2

  (C) 48, then add 2   (D) 48, then subtract 2

7. What is the missing digit? (Lesson 3.3)

$$
\begin{array}{r}
5,\ 3\ \ 2\ \ \boxed{} \\
+\ 3,\ 6\ \ \boxed{}\ \ 4 \\
\hline
\boxed{},\ 0\ \ 2\ \ 3
\end{array}
$$

  (A) 1   (B) 2

  (C) 5   (D) 9

8. There are four numbers on a whiteboard:

1,390, 1,125, 1,580, and 1,625.

The difference between two of the numbers is 235.

What are the two numbers? (Lesson 4.3)

  (A) 1,580 and 1,390   (B) 1,625 and 1,390

  (C) 1,390 and 1,125   (D) 1,580 and 1,125

9. How many numbers between 31 and 50 can be divided by 6 with no remainder? *(Lesson 8.4)*

(A) 1   (B) 2

(C) 3   (D) 4

10. Add 4,786 and 1,078. *(Lesson 3.3)*

(A) 3,708   (B) 3,808

(C) 5,764   (D) 5,864

11. Subtract 1,786 from 3,000. *(Lesson 4.3)*

(A) 1,204   (B) 1,214

(C) 2,786   (D) 4,786

12. 215 × 4 = _____. *(Lesson 7.3)*

(A) 172   (B) 211

(C) 219   (D) 860

13. Which of the following is the same as 5 × 9? *(Lesson 6.5)*

(A) 9 + 5   (B) 5 + 5 + 9 + 9

(C) 5 + 5 + 5 + 5 + 5   (D) 9 + 9 + 9 + 9 + 9

14. Drew has 87 pebbles.
He divides the pebbles equally into 3 bags.
How many pebbles does he have in each bag? *(Lesson 8.5)*

Ⓐ 29   Ⓑ 84

Ⓒ 90   Ⓓ 261

15. The sum of two numbers is 100.
The difference between the two numbers is 26.
What is the number that is less? *(Lesson 5.1)*

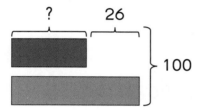

Ⓐ 13   Ⓑ 24

Ⓒ 37   Ⓓ 63

Short Answer

**Read the questions carefully.
Write each answer in the space provided.**

16. Write three thousand, fourteen in standard form. *(Lesson 1.1)*

_____

17. What is the value of the digit 5 in the number 5,631? *(Lesson 1.2)*

_____

18. Use the digits below to make three 3-digit odd numbers and three 3-digit even numbers. Do not repeat the same digits in a number. *(Lesson 8.3)*

1   8   2   3   9   4   7

Odd numbers: _____

Even numbers: _____

19. Add 1,850 + 59. *(Lesson 3.2)*

_____

20. $70 \times 4 = ?$ *(Lesson 7.1)*

_____

21. In $59 \div 2$, the quotient is _____, and the remainder is _____. *(Lesson 8.2)*

22. Shaun takes 300 photographs at the zoo.
Sheena takes twice as many photographs as Shaun.
How many photographs do they take in all? *(Lesson 9.1)*

_____ photos

23. Shannon has 78 animal stickers.
She has three times as many animal stickers as her brother, Ryan.
How many animal stickers does Ryan have? *(Lesson 9.3)*

_____ paperclips

24. The sum of two numbers is 1,500.
The difference between these two numbers is 300.
Find these two numbers from the numbers provided. *(Lessons 3.2 and 4.1)*

1,200   600   300   700   800   900

_____

25. Caroline packs some glue sticks into 8 bags.
She has 12 glue sticks left over.
If there are 25 glue sticks in each bag, how many
glue sticks did she have at first? *(Lessons 7.3 and 3.1)*

_____

Name: _____ **Date:** _____

26. What is the product of $1 \times 7 \times 2$?
Use the number lines to help you. *(Lessons 6.1 and 6.2)*

$1 \times 7 \times 2 = 1 \times$ _____

$= $ _____

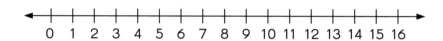

$1 \times 7 \times 2 = $ _____ $\times 2$

$= $ _____

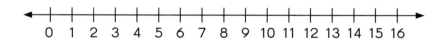

So, $1 \times$ _____ $= $ _____ $\times 2$

$= $ _____ .

27. Find the sum of 938 and 8,163. *(Lesson 3.3)*

_____

28. Find the difference between 6,215 and 8,356. *(Lesson 4.3)*

_____

29. Find the product of 154 and 4. *(Lesson 7.3)*

_____

30. Use the digits below to form two 2-digit numbers.
Each number has a remainder of 1 when divided by 4. *(Lesson 8.2)*

1   3   7   9

_____

31. Find the difference between $45 \div 5$ and 5×7. *(Lessons 4.3, 6.3, and 7.1)*

_____

© 2018 Marshall Cavendish Education Pte Ltd

32. Use the model. How many stamps does Alex have? *(Lesson 5.1)*

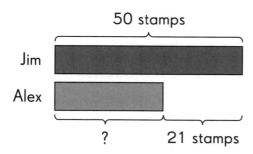

_____ stamps

33. A craft store sells 1,124 fewer pieces of red art paper
than blue art paper.
It sells 2,317 pieces of red art paper.
How many pieces of red and blue art paper does the craft store sell?
(Lessons 3.3 and 4.3)

_____ pieces

34. Ngu walks 250 feet.
She walks 65 feet more than Pauline.
How far does Pauline walk? *(Lesson 4.3)*

_____ feet

35. Oomi makes 4 necklaces.
She uses 156 beads for each necklace.
How many beads does she use in all? *(Lesson 7.3)*

_____ beads

Extended Response

Solve. Show your work.

36. Jolene has 600 wooden beads.
She has 285 fewer glass beads than wooden beads.

a. How many glass beads does Jolene have?

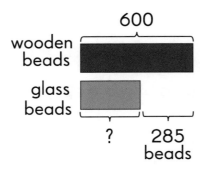

b. How many wooden beads does she have if she uses 150 of them to make necklaces?

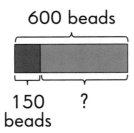

37. Company A gets 3,700 hits on their website.
Company B gets 450 fewer hits than Company A.

a. How many hits does Company B get?

b. How many hits do both companies get in all?

38. Noah swims 80 laps in 5 days.
He swims the same number of laps every day.

    a. How many laps does he swim in a day?

    b. How many laps does he swim in 4 days?

39. Jose has 88 stickers.
He puts 4 stickers on each bookmark.
He gives all his bookmarks away to his friends.
Each friend receives 2 bookmarks.

a. How many bookmarks does he put stickers on?

b. How many friends does he have?

40. A factory delivers 5 containers of pottery to a store.
Each container has 162 pieces of pottery.
The store owner discovers 24 pieces of pottery are broken.
How many pieces of pottery are not broken?